More Critical Praise

for *Face: One Square Foot of Skin*

"With her new book *Face: One Square Foot of Skin*, Justine Bateman . . . is trying to push back against the notion that women's faces are 'broken and need to be fixed' . . . [T]he book is a meditation on women's faces, and the cultural pressure to be 'ashamed and apologetic that their faces had aged naturally.'"
—*New York Times*

"There is nothing wrong with your face. At least, that's what Justine Bateman wants you to realize. Her new book, *Face: One Square Foot of Skin*, is a collection of fictional short stories told from the perspectives of women of all ages and professions; with it, she aims to correct the popular idea that you need to stop what you're doing and start staving off any signs of aging in the face."
—*W Magazine*

"[Bateman] studies the topic of women and aging in her new book *Face: One Square Foot of Skin*."
—*People*

"The actor and author of *Face: One Square Foot of Skin* wants to push back against the ubiquity of plastic surgery."
—*Vanity Fair*

"Through a selection of short stories, [Bateman] examines just how complicated it is for women to get older, both in and out of the spotlight."
—*Glamour*

"[Bateman is] putting an inspiring spin on aging by celebrating her face just as it is. Leaving us with an inspired State of Mind!"
—*Maria Shriver's Sunday Paper*

"I can't think of anyone better than Justine Bateman to start the conversation about how we've devolved into a society that doesn't allow women to age. Brave, brilliant, and unflinchingly honest, Justine is that writer you trust because she goes after every subject with a warrior's focus, and throws herself to the lions while she's at it. It doesn't hurt that she's a gorgeous woman who hasn't tried to erase an ounce of history from her face. I love the way she thinks, and am amazed at the many sublayers she manages to excavate while everyone else is scratching the surface."
—Mary-Louise Parker

"*Face: One Square Foot of Skin* [is] a creative nonfiction tome about the ways society responds to women as they age . . . [Bateman] said she was compelled to take a deeper look at the unfair expectations placed on women, particularly women in the public eye like her, as they grow older." —*Hollywood Reporter*

"Recent months have also seen a number of celebrities and other public figures speak out about embracing older skin. For example, in *Face: One Square Foot of Skin* . . . Justine Bateman explores women's relationships to their wrinkles . . . [Bateman's] message to readers is that they can interrogate these fears rather than feeling they have to alter their appearance to please someone else." —*Vox*

"Justine Bateman extends her creative talents to include fiction in this collection of vignettes that focus on how we've learned to react to women's faces as they age. Based on Bateman's own real-life interviews, the stories dig deep to uncover why we're uncomfortable with faces of a certain age, and argue that confidence—and not cosmetic procedures—are the answer to the problem."
—*Town & Country*, one of the Must-Read Books of Spring 2021

"Reading online comments about yourself can be a risky move, especially for those in the public eye. But for Bateman, it planted the seed for a hot-selling book and jump-started a candid conversation about outdated beauty standards and rampant ageism. And it all began when she typed her name into a search engine." —*Adweek*

"[Bateman] argues that American society has long equated the signs of aging on a woman's face with unattractiveness. But she also asserts that women need not participate in such prejudice by accepting and internalizing it." —*AARP*

"The message Bateman leaves us with is an important one. Basically, it is this: there's nothing wrong with your face."
—*Winnipeg Free Press*

"A much-needed viewpoint on an important and seemingly universal issue." —*Manhattan Book Review*

"This is what Bateman's book emphasizes—celebrate who you are, wrinkles and all." —*The Cyberlibrarian*

for *Fame: The Hijacking of Reality*

"Justine Bateman was famous before selfies replaced autographs, and bags of fan mail gave way to Twitter shitstorms. And here's the good news: she took notes along the way. Justine steps through the looking glass of her own celebrity, shatters it, and pieces together, beyond the shards and splinters, a reflection of her true self. The transformation is breathtaking. Revelatory and raucous, fascinating and frightening, *Fame* is a hell of a ride."
—Michael J. Fox, actor, author of
A Funny Thing Happened on the Way to the Future

"In *Fame: The Hijacking of Reality*, the two-time Emmy nominee takes a raw look at the culture of celebrity, reflecting on her stardom at its dizzying peak—and the 'disconcerting' feeling as it began to fade."
—*People*

"Wholly riveting."
—*New York Times Book Review*

"If you've ever dreamed of being famous someday, you need to read this book. If you've ever called a celebrity a 'has-been' or a 'flash in the pan' on social media, then you really need to read this book. Justine Bateman has crafted the most compelling and comprehensive treatise on the nature of fame that you're ever likely to read. Through a fearless act of self-examination, which she conducts with the scientific detachment of an anthropologist, Bateman illuminates both the short- and long-term effects of attempting to navigate the labyrinth of celebrity."
—Ernest Cline, author of *Ready Player One*

"Justine Bateman, in a voice both empathetic and take-no-prisoners, has produced a fascinating look at the psychology of present-day fame. She traces its roots down to humble beginnings in the injured psyche of every human, hoping to find a cure for what ails us all. In these early, heady days of the ascension of social media, in which everyone seems able to fulfill the Warholian dictum of fifteen minutes, Bateman casts a sober, never overly serious eye on today's media landscape and emerges without cynicism on the hard-won side of love and acceptance."
—David Duchovny, actor, author of *Miss Subways*

"A smart, unflinching, touching, riveting, one-of-a-kind hybrid of memoir and cultural analysis. Fame in its contemporary form is strange and powerful and deeply American; so is *Fame*."
—Kurt Andersen, author of *Fantasyland*

"Bateman digs into the out-of-control nature of being famous, its psychological aftermath and why we all can't get enough of it."
—*New York Post*

"The *Family Ties* alum has written the rawest, bleakest book on fame you're ever likely to read. Bateman's close-up of the celeb experience features vivid encounters with misogyny, painful meditations on aging in Hollywood, and no shortage of theses on social media's wrath." —*Entertainment Weekly*

"Bateman addresses the reader directly, pouring out her thoughts in a rapid-fire, conversational style. (Hunter S. Thompson is saluted in the acknowledgments.) . . . But her jittery delivery suits the material—the manic sugar high of celebrity and its inevitable crash. Bateman takes the reader through her entire fame cycle, from TV megastar, whose first movie role was alongside Julia Roberts, to her quieter life today as a filmmaker. She is as relentless with herself as she is with others."
—*Washington Post*

"In Justine Bateman's *Fame*, a deeply personal book about the *Family Ties* actor's experience in the limelight, she reminds us that famous people are exactly that: people." —*Guardian*

"You've never read anything quite like this book—don't call it a memoir—by the actress/director/producer best known for her role on the '80s sitcom *Family Ties*. It's a meditation on fame (if something so raw and full of expletives can be called a meditation), examining what it does to celebrities—and the rest of us."
—*Newsday*

"Walking through the familiar trappings of stardom—false friendships, abusive management, trust issues—Bateman underlines with grit the misconceptions of being a luminary which oft lead many to its pursuit." —*Women's Review of Books*

"Instead of crashing and burning, Bateman has found a life outside the maelstrom, ably described in this sharp, take-no-prisoners book." —*Kirkus Reviews*

"Bateman delivers a blisteringly honest analysis of fame and her years in and out of the spotlight . . . Bateman's impassioned narrative points out to those who relentlessly seek fame that rather than a blessing, it can be a curse." —*Publishers Weekly*

JUSTINE BATEMAN is a writer/director/producer with an impressive, decades-long résumé in film and TV that includes a Golden Globe nomination and two Emmy nominations. Bateman wrote and produced her directorial film short debut, *Five Minutes*, which premiered at the 2017 Toronto Film Festival and was chosen by seven more festivals, including the 2018 Tribeca Film Festival. *Violet*, Bateman's critically acclaimed directorial feature film debut of her own script, stars Olivia Munn, Luke Bracey, and Justin Theroux, and was an official selection at the 2021 SXSW Film Festival and the 2021 Toronto Film Festival. Her best-selling first book, *Fame: The Hijacking of Reality*, was published in 2018 by Akashic.

FACE

ONE SQUARE FOOT OF SKIN

JUSTINE BATEMAN

BROOKLYN, NEW YORK

Published by Akashic Books
©2021, 2022 Justine Bateman

Paperback ISBN: 978-1-63614-033-9
Hardcover ISBN: 978-1-61775-922-2
Library of Congress Control Number 2020947283

First paperback printing

Akashic Books
Brooklyn, New York
Instagram, Twitter, Facebook: AkashicBooks
E-mail: info@akashicbooks.com
Website: www.akashicbooks.com

To all the current and future "older broads" out there—may you always qualify for that honor

Introduction

When I was a smooth-skinned and plump-faced teenager, I really wanted to look like the older European actresses I saw in the Italian and French films of the 1960s and '70s. Chiseled cheeks, dark circles under their eyes, loose skin on the jawline, crow's feet framing the eyes. To me, these facial markings were the hallmarks of complex and exotic women, women with confidence and attitude and style, women who had no use for whatever you might think of them. Unfortunately, I was too young to have any of these interesting characteristics on my face. I longed for Jeanne Moreau's under-eye bags, Charlotte Rampling's sharp cheekbones and hooded eyelids, and Anna Magnani's deep and dark creases extending down from the inner corners of her eyes. I felt that if I had a face with those markings, people would immediately know I was interesting and complex; there would be no question.

I then grew older and I became more myself, with more of the traits I had admired about those older actresses. As luck would have it, my face changed accordingly. I was elated when creases emerged across the tops of my cheeks when I smiled, when

I saw the promising beginnings of small bags under my eyes, when the skin loosened on my neck. One summer, I even noticed a real bonus of "cleavage creases" on my upper chest from the sun. I was finally beginning to look like the kinds of women I thought were the most interesting, and the most attractive.

You can imagine how surprised I was to find that many people disagreed. I was taken aback to find that quite a few people had taken to Internet chat sites to passionately complain that "Justine Bateman looks horrible now." How was it possible that they didn't see what *I* saw on my face: the indication of a complex and exotic woman? How could it be that they saw the opposite of what I saw in my face?

This was confusing to process. (You can read more detail about that nauseating experience in my book *Fame: The Hijacking of Reality*.) But, on the other side of that process, I wanted to understand just how that passionately negative perception of an older woman's face exists in our current society.

Millions of other women have been eviscerated in this same way I was, via the loud and verbally vio-lent criticism of aging actresses, models, musicians, and politicians. This criticism filters down to *all* women, both in and out of the spotlight. For those *in* the spot-light, a panic can develop to surgically alter the aging face in an attempt to escape this "older, terrible face" criticism. For those *out* of the spotlight, there can be a bit of horror in watching those who were once lauded as some of the "most beautiful people" among us, publicly ripped to shreds when their faces age. Some of the thinking follows that if *those* "attractive" people aren't exempt from the criticism, and can now be drawn and quartered for looking older, what lies in wait for those with more "ordinary" faces?

A special terror is transmitted to younger women, teenagers, and girls. Yet still years away from experiencing any facial wrinkles or loose skin themselves, they can clearly see their trajectory in society as pigs-to-the-slaughter. Every year they inch closer and closer to being attacked themselves for their naturally aging faces. After all, not a week goes by without a girl hearing comments about older women like, "She used to be a looker, but she's really let herself go," "She looks like an old hag now," "Good thing she married before she lost her looks," etc. Comments like these constantly reaffirm that the girl has worth with an unlined and pretty face, but once that goes, she will be led into the slaughterhouse, like all the other older piggies. Unfortunately, when the girls look to the older women to see whether they are folding under that verbal pressure, or if they are instead boldly defying it with self-confidence, the girls more often see older women folding and rushing to surgically "fix" their faces. With few confident older female role models to counteract all the noise about their faces, one can hardly expect a relaxed attitude from any young female about the prospect of eventually looking older.

While I was still processing that "older face" criticism I personally experienced online, I wove in and out of adopting shame about my face when I interacted with others. And I noticed many other older women also looking shameful. Perhaps I was seeing shame in their eyes about something else in their lives, but it seemed too prevalent among a multitude of women of similar ages for that to be true. Averting the eyes when looked at, holding the mouth in a defeated angle, and even presenting a resigned posture appeared to be common among the older women I saw. I especially saw the shame because that was how I myself was feeling, or rather how I had decided to feel because others claimed my older face was "horrible." I was disturbed that not only had I bought into other people's critical idea of my appearance, but also that many women around me seemed to have done the same thing. I hated the idea that half the population was perhaps spending the entire second half of their lives ashamed and apologetic that their faces had aged naturally.

For me, it felt like a ploy to somehow shut me down, to get me to hide, to be quiet, to erase myself, all at the exact moment in my life when I had gained the most intelligence, the most wisdom, and the most confidence. What an easy way to try to make sure that I stopped accomplishing anything further. To keep me from enrolling in college, from writing books, from writing scripts, or from directing and producing films (all of which happened in the post-face-criticism years). In fact, what a perfect way to make sure *this* book never existed to tell you that the perception that your older face is "horrible" is just a lie you may have absorbed, and nothing more.

When observed at this angle, the focus on the female face seems to do nothing but severely distract females from achieving everything they were meant to. Traditionally, men's older faces signify power, and women's older faces signify a loss of power. What if this societal signaling has nothing to do with the idea of older men's superior ability to wield power, but has everything to do with women not sitting in their rightful places of power because they've folded under the weight of comments that they're no longer young and pretty looking? After all, we've long allowed the "pretty" compliment to be the ultimate female award, and in doing that we established that to be called "old and ugly" is the ultimate in female failure. With that sense of "failure," which older women are going to comfortably and confidently seek and sit in the power positions? On the surface, it may seem a small and silly reason for women to shy away from accomplishing things as they grow older, but a longer look will reveal it to be a pernicious distraction that has permeated seemingly every female fiber.

Do we naturally think this way about women's

older faces, or is it taught? If the definition of female "attractiveness" is tied to an unconscious, evolutionarily based desire to procreate and continue the species, then one can understand that the smooth, unlined faces that usually accompany women in childbearing years would be more "desirable" than creased faces, as the creased faces may indicate that a woman is in menopause and unable to breed any longer. Intellectually, we can see this, but with our population at over 7.6 billion people, and growing, wouldn't this be an outdated, vestigial concern in society? And it still doesn't explain the volatile emotions experienced by the older women, and by those who criticize their faces. Why the shame and why the anger?

I believe there are a multitude of causes for that shame and that anger, and very little of it rational. *Face* exposes some possible reasons and generally asks why we should ever find an older face "horrible" to begin with, and why would we feel compelled to "fix" it? It's a question that has been overlooked as society has become almost expectant about women employing the many means by which an older face can be "fixed."

Decades ago, the media, and women's fashion magazines in particular, used to reflect a society that looked askance at older women (and men) altering their faces with plastic surgery. There was a level of disgrace associated with it, and those who got their faces "lifted" were assumed to be desperate and vain. Aesthetically, plastic surgery results were rather obvious and the procedures were relatively uncommon. Years later, when other facial procedures became more prevalent, like fillers, Botox, and chemical peels, the magazines then started printing articles asking "should we or shouldn't we" use these methods. The decision seemed to fall heavily on the "yes, we should" side of the debate, and then gave way to a new discussion over exactly "which" techniques we should use. Once that was settled, informed primarily by the safety records of any given procedure, the new discussion developed as to exactly "when" to start using these methods. It was as if employing face-altering methods, now including the use of needles, knives, lasers, and acid, was the necessary responsibility of all women, and the only question left was, "Should you start employing these techniques around age 40, or should one start earlier, for the sake of 'maintenance,' at 30, or even at 20 years old?"

There were few, if any, simultaneous discussions in the public forum about the ethics of hammering women about the repellent nature of their naturally aging faces. No, this "fix it" position was presented to society as a fait accompli, and more than a little fueled in the women's fashion magazines by the pages and pages of ads purchased by an increasing number of facial-altering services, and "anti-aging" cream companies.

As we were busy leaping from information about one "breakthrough, face-altering procedure" to another, the one discussion that never took place was *why* did we think that older women's faces were something that need to be fixed at all, and what do we think "fixing" them will accomplish? And that's the discussion in which I'm most interested.

When I was deciding on a format for this book, I knew that as a reader I wouldn't want to read a mere academic look at the topic. I also wouldn't want to read something from just one person's perspective and experience. Rather, I wanted short narrative blasts into different experiences with older women's faces. And so, the book became 47 short stories in which I have incorporated my experiences and feelings on the topic, and those of about 25 people I interviewed. The interviewees were assured anonymity in order to encourage frank conversations for the book. All the emotions and events in the stories are true, wrapped in fictionalized names and circumstances.

Face is by no means an exhaustive exploration of "older women's faces" in our current society, but rather a series of snapshots that focus on the reasons for the negative attitudes regarding those faces. Actresses are represented here in larger numbers because they are the most common, and most violently subjected, targets of this negativity. Of course, there exist different attitudes toward women's faces aging, due to cultural or socioeconomic backgrounds, but drilling into those particular differences was not a focus of the book. Rather, *Face* focuses on that universal blanket that is laid over *all* older females related to their faces, regardless of whether that blanket affects a women only lightly, or completely smothers her ability to see herself properly. The stories expose some of the unspoken reasons there is so much hatred, from within and without, about women's older faces. My hope is that in exposing these reasons, they can wither and die in the light of day.

Because, in the end, there's nothing wrong with your face.

1

Tanya. 42. Actress.

The man drew a line with his finger from his mid-forehead down to the bridge of his nose, when he caught her eye. How long had he been trying to catch her eye? How long had he been thinking this? This admonishment of her, this warning, this "helpful hint"?

From the other side of the camera, she furrowed her brow, causing his anxiety to rise, she was sure. When she looked back later, she was sure.

Other people moved around her, working, setting the shot. She was an island, looking at this man on another island, and she saw him too clearly, no ocean haze to block his gesture.

Again his gesture. Again her brow furrow, her "Huh?"

Then, his finger wagging back and forth, once, twice.

Oh.

"Don't furrow your brow. Don't crease your skin. Don't move your forehead." That was the gesture, the metronome wagging of his finger.

The cinematographer on this TV show was bothered that she was using her forehead, or angry that she was creasing it, or confused as to how to light a forehead like this, she supposed. A forehead that had not known the puncture of a needle and the insertion of paralyzing toxins. A forehead that could still express confusion and contempt.

She wanted to make a scene. Wanting to make a scene for all the fashion magazines divesting themselves of the former plastic surgery stigma of years past and now instead pumping out article after article about plastic surgery in a matter-of-fact way. Making 20-year-olds and 50-year-olds and it-doesn't-matter-your-age adopt some assumption that everything on your face needs help. All that skin on your head, not covered in hair, needed something: an injection, a filler, an abrasive scrub, a cut-and-sew, a remedy.

Then she thought about all the face cream commercials on television, speaking to women, almost always. Speaking to women in a "helpful tone."

"We're just trying to help you. Don't worry. We're just trying to help you to not be seen in the hideous state you're currently presenting. Everywhere you go, people notice. They notice that you've failed. You've failed to maintain your looks, your appeal. Yes, we know you've raised a family on your own, or gotten your PhD, or are running a large company. But, let's be honest, none of that matters unless you have a fatigue-free, youthful-looking face. It just won't matter. But we're here for you. We can get you on the other side. Of the whispers-behind-the-hand comments, of that

'Hey guys, I don't mean any offense, I mean I really like her, but have you noticed that she's looking a bit jowly, a bit old now?' We're on your side."

She kept calm, calm for her. Out loud, though, she had to say something out loud. "What? Don't crease my forehead?"

He nodded affirmatively, relieved almost, that she understood his "note."

"Well, it's going to happen," she said flatly.

She wanted to vomit. No sickness, nausea, stomach issue, just an emotional relief gesture. Just vomit as a substitute for all the other things she wanted to say.

Goddamnit. A bit, a tiny bit, a little bit of panic now. She'd never heard that before, never, that "note." This show, though, most (all?) of the other actresses on this show had had toxic injections, partially paralyzing their faces. Disallowing their facial impulses from "damaging" their faces and putting them in a position to get comments, to have people whisper about them. Yes, maybe the cinematographer was confounded, having not lit or photographed a moving forehead in so long, confused about accommodating this anomaly.

That "note." She didn't want to think about it. "I'm strong. I look fine. He just doesn't know. He's too used to all the fakery. He just doesn't know."

But, she was thinking about it. It was in her stomach now, trying to lick her mind, trying to force its way up her throat and coat her mind with its spit while she was trying to concentrate on acting in the scene. Trying to act in the scene and not think about the finger that drew a line down the forehead and then wagged shame at her. Trying to not think about it now.

2

Faith. 48. Former Advertising Executive.

"Oh shit."

Faith jerked her head up so that her face was now perpendicular with the mirrored table she'd been cleaning, and not hovering over it, hanging over it.

"Oh shit."

She carefully looked down onto the reflective surface again. Skin sagged, pulled down, as if from a handful of delicate strings, pulled down toward the table.

"Oh God."

Had it happened? Was she now relegated to that category of women who are disdained, or who are supposed to feel disdained? She sat down on the couch. "Supposed to feel disdained." By whom? It suddenly seemed to her like some grand society-wide conspiracy. As if there were things she had to do when she reached a certain age: get an annual physical, start saving in earnest for retirement, treat yourself to a nice piece of jewelry, and start feeling ashamed about your face.

Faith sat there on the couch, looking out the window at the pool, the trees, seeing them, but not seeing them. She knew from her advertising days that people will accept what you tell them to accept. You tell them they have a flaw so you can sell them your remedy, the remedy they already didn't need. She remembered one particular account. Deodorant. The deodorant company was expanding into China and Faith had to solve the issue of the Chinese people apparently having little body odor. She had to develop an advance campaign to convince them that they stunk, so that the deodorant could be sold to them. And she did it. She crammed that idea right into the pores of millions of virtually odor-free Chinese people, such that they became appalled at their own nonexistent stench, and desperate to buy some deodorant to fix "the problem." Yeah, she was good.

She put her forehead in her hand. She unconsciously stretched the skin between her thumb and forefinger, gauging the degree of its slack.

"No," she said out loud, even, as she pulled her hand off her face. She had been a part of this manipulation of society; she had made a lot of money off it. She knew how it all worked, so why was she herself feeling subject to it?

The older female face: the sea hag; the evil witch; the loving but ineffectual grandmother; the mean schoolteacher; the domineering matron; the spinster; the bordello madam; the discarded first wife; the boss (who's a bitch).

The younger female face: Hope! Fun! Adores

you! Life! Fruitfulness! Joy! Acceptance! Freedom! Sex! Permissiveness! Easily impressed! Grateful! Dependent!

Goddamnit, she knew this, she knew the tropes, the symbolism. She had used them all in her ad campaigns. But now. Now. Wait. Goddamnit. Her mind felt like mush. She shook her head a little bit, as if that would clear it.

"I don't have to buy into this. I don't have to." She knew her face was no different there on the couch than it had been an hour ago, when she'd felt fine, before she saw the skin fall almost toward the mirrored tabletop. But, it wasn't an hour ago; she had since seen that her face had crossed over.

Maybe others had already noticed and she was only now just realizing. She felt parts of her brain closing, like shutters slapping closed in the first strong breeze of a tropical storm. Not there yet, but inevitable. She tried to stop the shutting, to reverse it. Shutters to windows she'd had open her whole life: attractiveness to men, others' willingness to listen to her in meetings, favored treatment, even just basic confidence. She couldn't stop the slamming of the shutters. The mountain of tropes and symbols were etched so far into her head that the shutters acted independently of her own intellect and reason. She couldn't stop it.

She went back to cleaning the table, careful not to look down now at the string-pulling of her skin to the mirror. She knew. She knew that she'd be unable to shake this when her kids returned from school later, when her husband came home from work tonight. She would look into their eyes and be convinced that they, too, knew she'd crossed over. And that she could never go back.

3

Denise. 50. Housekeeper.

"Jesus, she's really let herself go."

She didn't look up, didn't need to look up, from her buttered toast and her grapefruit juice.

"She really screwed the pooch," he went on. "She'd be lucky if me or my boys would ever touch her now. Jeez. What a waste."

She didn't need to look up to know he was talking about a stranger: an actress, a singer maybe. Someone they didn't know, had never met.

There was something about this time, though, the criticism this time, that made Denise decide to finally look up at her husband. Sitting there in his chair at the breakfast nook. His computer open in front of him. Looking at what? *People.com?* No, someone must have forwarded him something, e-mailed him some woman's picture. Some guy from his office, some e-mail with a bunch of other guys on it, a big group e-mail so they could circle-jerk all the comments about some actress who'd probably just turned 40.

It was the "lucky if we would touch her now" part. That part, that made her look up at her husband. And not as his wife, not as someone who really knew him, knew his heart and all that crap, but just looked. Flashy shoes (always), cheap corduroys, pot-belly, ill-fitting T-shirt, short stature, thinning hair. Skin drooped from his eyes and his cheekbones, places where youthful fat used to fill out. None of that really bothered her before, but now. The comment, as if a woman is always wanting and available to all men. As if whether or not a woman would sleep with a man is up to the man. As if her husband and his similarly jowly and misshapen coworkers can have any woman at all, but would reject those who are blemished or "past their prime."

"I wouldn't do her now. Nope!" As if, that's it. The woman had exhausted her allotment of appeal, and the man, forever appealing, forever a "catch," forever in a "buyer's market" for female meat, had noticed this and had turned her out.

She felt a stump of affection for him now.

4

Tessa. 45. Postal Worker.

Tessa looked over at her boyfriend, Sam. Same age. Same damn age. But he didn't seem bothered by, concerned with, hindered by, his aging face. Total confidence. Total confidence. She caught herself marveling. He laughed at something Curt said to him. Pushing the hamburgers around on the grill, Sam laughed. Big and loud, Sam let his amusement splinter the skin on his face with twenty wrinkles, maybe more. Not a concern in the world. Smoke and heat from the barbecue drifting up and over Sam's face as he wiped a laughter tear from his left eye, carelessly wiped that delicate skin around the eye.

Tessa looked away, toward the clutch of pine trees at the edge of their lawn. She wanted to die. Not die, but just be out of this bullshit. The money she'd spent on face creams and salon facials. Never getting fillers or injections or surgery. Not even a laser resurfacing, like Suzanne was always excitedly telling her to get. Not even the latest, the "Vampire Facial." Sounded disgusting anyway. She just wanted out from giving a shit. She wanted to be like Sam.

She looked back at him, now over at the dessert

table, where he was half-thinking about sticking his finger into the side of the cake to taste the frosting. He would too, before the afternoon was done. She knew that. He was intently listening to some woman, Geraldo's wife maybe, telling him some story. Her, with her bright face, emoting, but not showing it in her forehead or at the sides of her eyes. Emoting and needing to rely on the tenor of her voice to really get her emotional point across, because her facial expressions were handicapped by Botox. Sam seemed to have taken the emoting baton from her, furrowing his brow with empathy for what she was saying but couldn't really express with her own face.

Tessa was used to faces like Geraldo's wife's; that wasn't what was holding her attention. It was Sam's furrowed brow and his lack of concern about it. His brow was double-furrowed at this point, furrowed for him and furrowed for Geraldo's wife, and Tessa knew it was not going to affect how anyone treated him in a store, how anyone related to him at work, nor how any of his buddies looked at his face. Not only were those deep lines between his eyebrows not going to change how others saw him, they were not going to change how Sam saw himself. And that, *that* was what Tessa wanted. Goddamnit, that was what she wanted.

5

Nina. 24. Hairdresser.

Nina liked traveling alone. She could stay where she wanted, see what she wanted, leave town whenever she liked. She was stylish, confident, attractive. She knew it, she used it, why not. Today's plan was to leave her tiny attic hotel room (absolutely perfect, by the way) in the completely charming seaside town there in southern France and take the train up to Nice, just to walk around, maybe buy some more English-language books. She knew she should be making more of an effort to read books in French, but she felt lazy about it.

She quickly took the two flights of stairs down to the lobby and smiled slyly to the desk clerk as she passed, and then to the doorman as he opened the heavy wooden door for her. As she walked to the train station, she caught her reflection in the window of the bakery. She smiled to herself at her ability to capture the right amount of insouciance or careless-ness in her outfits. The right amount of wear and tear, the right combination of garage-sale finds and de-signer touches, the right timing ahead of the current trends. Perfectly orchestrated clothing, of course, but damn, she had it down. She knew it: a real "It Girl."

She reached the train just in time. The conductor eagerly, unnecessarily, helped her up the two steps into the train car. She looked back over her shoulder, after, and smiled a "merci." The ride was uneventful, not even anyone for her to flirt with, just the rhythmic clapping of the steel train wheels over the rail joints. Click. Click. Click. Click. Click. Click.

On the Nice train platform, she used some of her French to ask a baggage handler about a bookstore. He wasn't much help, but he smiled and flirted and shyly tried out some of his English on her. The exchange suited Nina's purposes, a general direction for the bookstore and some nice attention. Out in the street, she liked the smells of both the ocean and the bigger city mixed together. Nina walked down the sidewalk, pretty pleased with herself and with the way the flounce of her skirt played up and down. She came close to the square with maybe a bookstore, the one she thought the baggage handler mentioned, when she suddenly stopped.

A woman. A woman was half-jogging over to a waiting car. Her short boots were gray suede with little spiked heels and gray suede straps wrapped and tied around the ankle. Her jeans were tight to her calves and half-pushed into her boots. Her white T-shirt was on the verge of threadbare and it seemed indecisive about staying on her left shoulder. When the woman got to the car, the T-shirt's wide collar slid down the shoulder finally, revealing the strap of a purple bikini top.

Nina was taken with the woman's style. She started walking over, closer to the postcard kiosks, to get a better look, to see the woman from another angle, to really take in her look, make mental notes: the hair, the jewelry, everything. The woman was now leaning on the open driver's window, talking to the driver, both of them murmuring in French. Nina couldn't make it out, the French was too fast and low for her to translate. It didn't matter. The woman's belt was studded here and there with brass rivets. It was the kind of belt some kid in the 1950s would have used to play cowboys and Indians. The woman had four thin gold bracelets on her right arm and a ball-bearing chain wrapped a few times around her other wrist. Two turquoise rings were heavy on her fingers. This woman had "it." Nina wanted this. It wasn't just the look, it was the confidence, the way this woman moved. It was all of it. The woman then tossed her long, glossy, brown hair to the other side and Nina saw her face for the first time. Older. Much older. 50, 55, Nina figured.

"Holy shit."

Nina's mind went blank, and then almost immediately filled again. The woman's older face made this whole look. This confidence, the clothes, the jewelry, the way she half-jogged to the car—all of it

. . . The woman's face made it all beyond style. Her face seemed like some giant "fuck you" to society, to the way women were "supposed to be" at that age. But, shit, maybe that was just America and not here. Not here, at all. Nina was not in Boston anymore. She knew this. She knew this already, of course. But this really felt like somewhere else, a place where the women weren't conditioned after 45 or so to turn in their personalities in exchange for some "older woman" character. All the women Nina knew back home, or even at her dad's place in Virginia, had given themselves over to "older woman" characters. They all seemed like they'd handed over their own personalities, the ones that had started when they were girls and then developed in college, and were on the verge of becoming full-blown during their first marriage engagement, but then stopped, when? After the first baby was born? Or sooner? When the pregnancy started? The divesting, the women letting go of their own continuous progress and development and evolution of their personalities, for what? Societal acceptance? Just tossed into the trash. Nina could never square those women with their pasts, with their histories. The "Oh yeah, I went to Duke" or the "Sure, I rode horses competitively and almost made it to the Olympics," with who these women were now in their late 40s or 50s or beyond. Resigned and resembling each other, not just in looks, but attitude, behavior, as if all the individuality had been forfeited somehow.

"Holy shit."

The woman kissed the man in the car on one cheek and then the other. He said something else to her as he started to drive away and the woman put on her black, squared, oversized sunglasses.

"Ciao, bella!"

"Ciao!"

This woman had done it. She had stayed herself or become herself, Nina didn't know which. But she was there. She was bulletproof. She couldn't be touched. By not divesting her personality, by not becoming what society would expect, she was not subject to its rules, almost. Maybe here, in Nice, they didn't expect this divestiture of personality, Nina didn't know. But for all her own confidence and style and orchestrated look, Nina knew the ultimate accessory was going to be an older face. She knew now that there was nothing that special about walking around with style and confidence and a smooth 24-year-old face and body. But to have that style when people think you shouldn't, to have that confidence at an age when no one expects it, to not follow any unwritten personality divestiture rules, that was something. Nina knew that pairing the style and the confidence with a creased face was going to be her greatest head-turner.

6

Anne. 35. Music Teacher.

"I can't let you in because you're as old as fuck . . ."

She couldn't hear the rest of the line, the rest of the line that the nightclub doorman was saying in the film to the woman. To Leslie Mann, the actress, playing the woman whose name Anne couldn't remember.

"You're old as fuck . . ."

Leslie Mann's face was completely unlined. She was maybe 32? Anne couldn't really tell.

"Old as fuck . . ."

The doorman didn't know her, but he was looking at her. Looking at her. Saying this because he was looking at her.

"Old as fuck."

Leslie Mann looked younger than Anne, younger by five years, ten years. Younger, but "old as fuck."

Anne felt shame bloom in her, in a rush. Involuntarily, she turned slightly from her friend, there next to her in the movie theater. Simone, relaxed in her red, plaid flannel shirt, slouched in the burgundy, velveteen-covered theater seat. Probably smiling to herself or chuckling a little at the scene. Anne didn't want to look, didn't want the light of the screen to

catch her own eyes as she grabbed a furtive, sideways glance to see if Simone, even Simone, was
laughing, smiling, amused by the scene.

Anne felt a little nauseous. Too much popcorn,
or she shouldn't have let that tall concession guy put
on two layers of butter (or artificial butter, she didn't
know anymore), or she shouldn't have eaten the almost burnt, crunchy kernels at the bottom of the tub,
like she always did. Her tongue started patrolling her
teeth at the thought of that, in search of an errant
kernel shell between them, or one carefully wedged
in the gum line like a stem in a Japanese flower
arrangement.

"Old as fuck . . ."

Maybe the bouncer said something else after
that, something conciliatory, something to soften the
blow, or to excuse it, but Anne couldn't hear the dia-
logue anymore. Leslie Mann was sitting on the curb
now? Crying about something? Crying about her
"old as fuck" face?

Anne felt angry. Leslie Mann playing the sibling.
The one who can give advice to her newly pregnant
sister. And because she's not younger than the newly
pregnant sister, because she's not a teenager, she's
"old as fuck"? Anne was missing some of the plot
that followed; her head felt noisy, like a radio not
quite tuned in to the station, like on a road trip when
you've driven out of range of the stations in the town
you just left.

Anne was gently crushing a found kernel shell between two of her teeth on the right side of her mouth when Simone suddenly nudged her and laughed at something else on the screen, in the dark movie theater, with other people laughing at this thing, this new thing in the film. Anne smiled gamely back and as she did, she wondered, for the first time in her life, if she looked "old as fuck" doing that, smiling gamely back. Did she look that way to Simone there, or to the tall concession worker who pumps too much butter on the popcorn, or to everyone she'd seen in the past year? She now hated this film's writer, this director, these actors, this scene for taking her there, for "informing" her, for making everyone around her—she was convinced now—think that someone with a face as unlined as Leslie Mann's was "old as fuck." To condition them to think that. And Anne, with more than a few more lines than Leslie Mann, was then more than "old as fuck." At 35, her well had been poisoned.

7

Gina. 44. Author.

This face.

What did it represent?

That was the crux of it, wasn't it?

Gina looked closer at herself, moved closer to the bathroom mirror. She was safe and provided for, between the bathroom's white, veined marble walls and floors, the modern brass fixtures. Silk and cashmere and lace and vintage denim in the closet. Linen T-shirts, appropriately soft and worn and expensively slouchy. Her time was her own. Writing her spy novels at whatever pace she felt. Husband attentive, loving, present. Cars, her favorite, a BMW, in the garage.

This face, though, was not the face she wanted.

She'd resisted, so far, resisted all that her friends had done to their faces. Holly, who spent over $2,000 a month on face creams and treatments, expenses she always asked the salon to scatter about on the account, call them other things, to hide them from her husband. "Say I got a massage, a few pedicures. He doesn't get it, you know?" Or Lily, who nipped and tucked and still feared she'd be "accused" somehow, that some sagging or wrinkled part of her face that she missed or that had cropped up through the surgically tended field would be pointed out by a stranger, or worse, someone she knew. That she would become fodder for criticism, like the criticism Lily herself constantly shoveled onto others. "Judge not lest ye be judged." Gina knew that didn't mean that others were going to judge you, but that you were going to terrorize yourself with the same criticism you had heaped on others. You were going to treat yourself the same way.

What was so wrong with her face then? Older, OK, but did that really bother her? It represented, though, it represented, what? Gina started brushing her hair too roughly. She stopped. She didn't want to think about this today. This thought, the question about representation . . . She could feel her spy-novel-conspiracy-theory-plot-heavy-character-detailed head start the motor, though. It started digging, as if she were one of her own characters, her author mind looking for the motivation, to discover why this character of "Gina" didn't like her face. Why she used to like her face, but now didn't like her face.

Gina moved into the bedroom and resigned herself to the treasure hunt upon which her mind had just decided.

"Shit . . . OK, OK." She sat on the bed, the too-hard bed her husband loved, insisted on. The bed she'd gotten used to and had caused her to now take umbrage at softer beds at the hotels they visited.

Her face now represented . . . failure.

Gina furrowed her brow. How was that the right answer? Her mind raced to when she'd last felt "success," the opposite of failure, the opposite of this feeling. 24 or so. Two years out of college and publishing her first novel. 24. Exhilarated by that first success, blasted by it really, in a way she would never feel again, no matter the level of success since. She hadn't expected it, hadn't been looking for it, hadn't been chasing it. But, like a good drug, it made Gina chase it over and over, afterward. And like an addictive drug, made Gina grab more and more to feel the same way as the first time. Like the low one-tablet, recommended Advil dosage that only ever worked the first time and never again after your system grew accustomed to it. Gina couldn't feel less than a four-tablet dose anymore.

She got up and walked to her closet, eyeing the clock on the dresser. She was getting somewhere with the digging. She knew this feeling from all the characters she'd written, getting close to the "nut" of the character. White cotton blouse and charcoal slacks. She pulled on the slacks and took the blouse off the hanger. This outfit, this standard "I know what I'm doing" for today's meeting with that bookstore chain. That sweaty-palm-shaking and I-can't-wait-to-wash-my-hands-now and for-God's-sake-don't-touch-your-face-or-mouth-until-after-you-wash-your-hands-in-the-lobby-at-the-end meeting.

24-year-old success. OK, so wanting her face to look like that again to recapture that feeling. Sure, she saw that; it was obvious, too obvious really, for any character she would write. Too pat, too easy. Her phone was vibrating on the bedside table. Bra and slacks, checking the caller ID. Her husband. She let it go to voice mail. Looked at the time. Late, getting late. Buttoning the blouse, while one foot turning shoes around to get them on, to get out the door. Her mind turning still, like swimming pool towels in a dryer. She stopped. Just one shoe on now, she knew to let the thoughts turn.

Then a realization, almost subrealization. The connection before, the one she thought was so obvious, so pat, too pat for one of her books, the one about her "wanting to look like she did when she was 24, because that would act as a time-traveling device that would cause the whole successful situation to return," deflated suddenly. The subrealization was Gina remembering that she'd never noticed her looks before, that her success had never been tied to her looks. She was attractive and young then, sure, but nothing about her success at 24 was tied to her having an attractive, unlined, youthful face. Nothing about it. So, that "understanding" before, that irrational assumption that looking 24 would time-travel her back to that success, was negated now.

She knew she could never explain to her friends, who placed almost their entire worth on the evenness of their faces. But this subrealization pulled something off Gina. If that first rush of success and feeling that she could do no wrong was in no way related to her face, then the age in her face now just didn't matter. The lines or lack of lines mattered as little now as they had then. What she really wanted now was that freedom, that happiness, that low level of expectation wherein any accomplishment would thrill her.

It felt like a new problem, she knew, as she grabbed her car keys downstairs in the kitchen. A new problem, where she was going to have to square her current success with whatever drug-like high she remembered from the first success, to make her current successes as satisfying. At least, though, she wasn't going to have to criticize her face. She was never again going to have to think that this wasn't the face she wanted. She was not going to have to do that again.

8

Donna. 48. Actress.

"Holy shit, she's here."
"She came!"
"She was seriously in your class?"
"Donna Weston? You know her?"
"Steve, go say something. You had drama club with her, right?"

Donna heard them. She could always hear them. Right near her, as if they thought she was deaf. Or far away; she could still hear them.

Better to battle the enthusiasm with enthusiasm.

"Hey, fuckers! What's going on?!"

"Oh my God! I haven't seen you in 30 years! I mean, I've seen you in all your films and everything, but wow, you came!"

"I figured if I was going to come to one of the class reunions, it would have to be the last one. I mean, they don't do any more after 30. Do they?"

"I don't know, but it's so great to see you!!"

"I'm Chris Thompson's wife, Kiki. Hi! I just have to ask, is Brad Pitt nice in real life?"

"C'mon, Kiki, what the hell?"

"It's OK. He is, he is . . ."

And so on.

Donna knew it would be like this. It's OK. Answer a few questions, let people get over the shock of being in the same room as her, let them finally remember her as just one of their classmates from years ago. That was why she came after all, to try to feel some of that normalcy. Even if it felt like she was touching it through Saran Wrap, just on the other side of a 30-year chasm that was now filled with her glittering, impossible fame.

She got there, she got some of that. Some of that "You're looking fine, Weston . . ." from the now-49-year-old, still-good-looking wide receiver of the 1988 Telles Creek High School football team. Some of the hugs that are always accompanied by a shrill "Oh my God!" from her old girlfriends. Some of the "Congrats!" and all that from her old classmates. It was good. Even with the occasional autograph requests and old friends who just couldn't get past her status in Hollywood now. Even with that.

Then a break. By herself out in the hall by the lockers, beyond the dark-green double doors with the reunion party pounding behind her, she was almost stunned that hallway smelled the same. She turned to trace the well-worn path to the bathrooms.

She could hear some guys talking up ahead,

around the corner. One voice sounded something like Mike Fuller, her old junior year science lab partner. Just as she neared the corner of lockers, she realized they were talking about her. She stifled a giggle and stood still, there, hidden.

"Yeah, Donna!"
"Can't believe she came."
"She was very pretty when I was 17 years old. What the hell happened?"

Oh shit. This wasn't what she . . . This wasn't what she thought she'd be hearing.

"Well, you're not 17 years old now, are you?"
"Drugs."
"Ditto."
"Woof."

Oh fuck. Drugs? Like she looked like she did drugs? Seriously?

"In all fairness, her look isn't the most flattering. With some makeup and her hair done I would bet she isn't that bad. More importantly, you think she's making any money off residuals? I have a real desire to be a kept man."
"Has she turned 50?"
"She found liberal veganism."

"Don't the films actually have to be aired to pay?"
"The top and bottom halves of her face look like they belong to completely different people. WTF?"
"And drugs."
"We're all getting older."
"That's weird. Usually women get more attractive as they get old. So bizarre."

Someone, she didn't know the voice, she didn't know who was defending her with the sarcasm. She felt like she was in some parallel universe. Sure, she'd had criticism from the press at times and online comments, which she tried her best to ignore, but these were people she knew, people who were just 20 minutes ago fawning all over her.

"I think the films are being aired somewhere."
"'Bout to say, she looks like a lot of moms I see at my kids' school or sports stuff. She's not made up to go out on a date. She looks like she's waiting for her daughter's dance practice to end. Would hit it, for sure."
"As picky as you are, that's saying something."
"I was about to say the same thing. He's known for being very selective."

Was that Nick Goldstein? Fuck. She couldn't tell. Maybe. Her heart was starting to skip a beat or two. No, no, no, not that. She tried breathing more steadily, to stop the heart palpitations.

"She isn't Hollywood Attractive, but she probably looks better for her age than most here."
"Bitch got da AIDS!"
"She looks like Steven Tyler after a relapse on Peruvian coke."

A hard laugh. A horsey laugh. Didn't she know him? Oh God, oh God, the things they were saying. Did they mean it? Or was this some male-male posturing? DID THEY ACTUALLY MEAN IT?

"She looks like she started taking testosterone shots."
"Age for the win and still undefeated . . . By the way, she still looks better than if she had fucked herself up with all that plastic surgery, trying to pretend she wasn't getting older. I would hit it."
"I'm confused. I think she looks pretty good for her age."

Another defense, but she could barely hear it. Her blood was throbbing in her ears now. She made her breaths longer to not pass out, to not let the panic run through her again. Please, not here, not here. Not where these men would have to be the ones to carry her out to some car, or some ambulance to have a "lie down" and some intravenous fluids. Not here.

"It's just age, I never thought she was a smoke show when she was young though."

"It's different when you're 16. She was wholesome, decent-looking."

"Looks like another bad case of global warming."

"Seriously. At 50, your fuckability isn't the same as 20."

"And that's a damn shame really. Wish we could Benjamin Button that shit and be hot as fuck when we knew what we were doing."

"Speak for yourself."

"You lacked the perspective that an adult has. Ask people to rate her at her ideal age. I bet you get no ratings above 7.1."

She wanted this to end. Please, to end.

"And most people will demand to see the body, legs, ass, all that."

"She turned into PJ Harvey."

"I think she's one of the coolest chicks around. Would marry her, even if time has not been as kind to her as it has been to some."

Their voices drifted off, they were walking away, down the hall, away. Donna was shivering. The blood still beating in her ears. She knew she had to sit, get to a seat, let this pass. Just get to the bathroom and let it pass. Let the panic press out.

Her vision started to get a bit blurry. It wasn't too bad, not terrible yet. It would be OK, if she could sit for a while. It was going to be OK. The bathroom door was there now, blue paint covering the wood, cool on her hand as she shoved the girls' door open. Mercifully, no one was in there. She almost fell into the stalls as she tried walking the length of the tiled floor, but stopped at the second-to-last stall. That was OK. It was far enough.

Lock the door, sit on the toilet. Head between the knees. Breathe, breathe. Head below the heart, for the blood. Then some tears. She didn't know how they could have been saying those things. So freely, so certainly.

Donna heard the bathroom door slapped open and a stream of voices poured in. A couple of women into the first stalls, the rest at the sinks, the mirrors. Just by sound, Donna figured where they were standing. She'd just sit there, in the second-to-last stall, and wait. She'd get better, get the blood to stop, and wait for the women to leave.

"I've seen all her films. I mean all of them."
"Even . . ."
"Yeah, of course!"
"Well, she didn't age well."
"She's only 48, she's probably a smoker."

Oh fuck.

"Her eye makeup is not good and she looks like she

has smoker's lines on her face, but other than that, she looks like a normal 48-year-old."

"I think we are so used to celebrities with massive plastic surgery, we are not used to seeing what actual aging looks like."

"I don't think she looks bad here, but when she was in that film . . ."

"I think it may be just because of the severity of the hair pulled back and the thick black eyeliner that makes her look a bit harsh tonight. I think she just needs someone to show her how to apply her makeup a bit better and maybe a more flattering hairstyle and she would be fine."

Wow, wow.

"I think she looks rather good for her age."

"No plastic surgery."

"She hasn't had any."

"And she smokes."

"The most wooden actress around."

"She looked bad at 30. Now, she just looks like hell."

"Donna looks really bad."

"She really does."

"I think she's had a lifelong eating disorder."

"Oh my."

"I know, she looks rough."

"We're the same age."

"Here, look at her in this picture."

What was happening? Was this some *Twilight Zone* experience, some practical joke? She supposed a phone had been whipped out at the sinks, some search had been feverishly conducted about her face, and the perfect photos had been found on-line. Donna felt a stab of nausea and closed her eyes.

"She looks fine, but the lighting's bad."
"It's because she had no work or Botox done."
"Aw!"
"Finally, an actress who looks her age!"
"That is not what 48 looks like! I am only 8 years from that?"
"Yes."
"Heck no!!! Here is one instance where being black is an advantage."
"Ha ha."
"Yeah, this is 48 on a white woman."
"Holy earth mama."
"She aged. "
"Wow, maybe drugs or anorexia. Or she just doesn't Botox like everyone else and we've forgotten what 48 looks like."
"I'm 48 and I don't look like that. I don't mean to be snarky."

Fuck. Fuck. She couldn't recognize any of the voices.

Were any of them classmates? Were they all wives of her classmates?

"Or . . . you THINK you don't look like that."
"I know. I must have good genes. No one believes my age."
"I don't mean to be snarkier, but you do look like that. That's what most real women look like at this age. It's just hard to see it in yourself."
"Then everyone is lying to me when they say I don't look my age. Or when they tell my husband he is a lucky man."
"You are so funny."
"Yes! I do have a great sense of humor. Everyone says that too."
"I know a lot of 48-year-olds, non-Botoxed ones, and she looks rougher than most."
"She looks normal. Just not a lot of makeup, and an awkward expression, and no fake tan so she doesn't look the way you expect a celeb to."

Defense, and then the stab. Donna felt the panic start to subside. Now, she just felt sad and mad and confused. She carefully leaned her head down, below the toilet bowl, to see out under the stall door.

"Right."
"I had the same reaction when I saw that photo be-

fore. She lives in LA, so there's sun damage, no plastic surgery, no Botox."

"Holy crap."

"She looks closer to 60."

"It says she's 42 here."

"She looks like a witch!"

"Happy Halloween!"

"42 . . ."

"Yeah, she was lookin' old already in that one film a few years ago."

"Is she a smoker or drug addict??"

"I don't think she looks so bad."

"Merciful heavens! I'm three years older and I KNOW I don't look like that. First of all, eyebrows . . ."

A couple of stall doors clicked open, more footsteps, more women to "weigh in." Donna could see that one of the women wore a pair of high emerald-green pumps. They rushed forward as she spoke.

"Oh my! She looks awful."

"I think it's a combination of really bad lighting and shoddy makeup."

"And she's not doing the plastic surgery, professional eyebrows, and hair jobs, either."

"I really like her—so shocked Donna hasn't aged better."

"She's too skinny, plus maybe alcohol and cigarettes."

"Yeyo too."

"Do you mean coke?"
"You know—I bet she just hasn't had the work done that other actresses have had . . . Our view of aging is so distorted now."
"Everyone has had work done now, and we are so confused about what older women look like."

The defenses felt dull and leaden to Donna now. She didn't even hunger for them any longer.

"She looks about average for her age, I think. Average in normal-person terms, not Hollywood terms."
"I totally agree."
"I totally agree, but still think she looks terrible."
"I totally agree. I think she looks fine."
"Yup, and this photo is not photoshopped and Vaseline-lensed."
"Almost all red carpet/pap photos we see are. They only aren't when the publications want to make a point."
"Exactly. We are being manipulated at their discretion."
"For the 'Stars Without Makeup!' bumper issues. I wouldn't be famous for all the tea in China. What a living nightmare."
"I totally agree. I was too bored to say it, but now I will—I think she looks GREAT!"
"Maybe if she gained a few pounds?"
"She got all religious and fuddy, I think. Maybe that did it."

"I thought she went Scientology?"

"Same diff."

"That's even worse."

"She was in the last few scenes of that superhero film and she looked like hell. I was shocked she didn't do better maintenance."

"Am I insane? I think she looks pretty frigging awesome."

"I totally agree. Cool and natural."

"I agree with you. Lovely eyes."

"Me too! I mean, she's 48. If she were going to look any younger, she'd look—well, fake and younger. She looks 48, but a hot 48, and what more can you ask for?!"

"GET OUT! Who thinks she looks bad? Her forehead is flawless, eyes are beautiful, and the only thing I see is laugh lines around her mouth. What the fuck?"

"She doesn't look 20, so therefore she's ugly and serves no purpose. Didn't you get the memo?"

"I'm 40, and I'd love to look this good at 48. Honestly, some of my friends who are 42/43 look like this now."

"I agree, I thought the same thing."

"She is not a hot 48."

"WHAT? Show me a hot 48-year-old, then."

"The makeup is all wrong on her."

Finally, mercifully, their voices became more faint. They filed out. Donna took a big breath that didn't clear out any of it. Burning in her brain, embers of

horror, or a structure of some other plane of existence where she's ugly and everyone disdains her.
She pressed her hands against her face. She had
to leave the reunion. Could she forget this? She assumed she would, but knew she could not. She knew
this would never leave her. Shit.

She reached back and flushed the toilet out of
some habit of justification and opened the stall door.
She stood at the sink and let the cold water run over
her fingers. In the hall, later, the green double doors
to the gym were open, music sloppily spilling into the
hallway. People had migrated out near the lockers,
too.

As Donna neared, that familiar wave of fame rec-
ognition speared every single person. They aborted
their conversations, they stood up straighter, they
put brighter looks on their faces.

"Hey, Donna! You look like you're heading out!"

"You know how it is . . . !"

"Donna, Donna. I don't know if Kevin . . . I'm Kevin
Terance's wife, Ginger. You guys worked in the at-
tendance office together senior year. He talks about
you, and I just want to say what a huge fan I am. I
mean, I just love what you do. Open door if you ever
want to come over for a drink. You know, if you want
to take a break from the whole Hollywood scene . . ."

"Well thank you. That's so nice of you." Donna
glanced down. At the emerald-green pumps. The
emerald-green pumps on Ginger. "Ginger?"

"Yeah! That's right."

"Ginger, when you're going to rip someone open, check under the toilet stall doors first."

Ginger was genuinely confused. "Pardon?"

"Your shock that I haven't aged better?"

Ginger blinked and tilted her head to the side. Maybe she was starting to tune out, starting to leave her body. "Oh . . . Donna . . ."

Donna leaned in. "Ginger, fuck you." She turned and continued down the hallway.

Then she heard that laugh, that horsey laugh from before. She turned her head fast and saw that it really was Mike Fuller, her old junior year science lab partner. Donna rubbed her forearm and felt her chest depress. Though she wanted to walk away and start to forget it all, she walked toward him instead, to finish this. His eyes lit up when he saw her approach, just like she knew they would.

"Donna! Holy shit! You look amazing! Man! I haven't seen you in 25 years! You've been killing it. Can't believe you'd come see us. This is the best!"

"Mike. Mike. We had such a good . . . In school, we were buds."

Mike looked surprised, but just for a moment. "Yeah, yeah! Of course. We had a blast in lab."

Donna looked at him for a beat. "Did you come up with that Steven Tyler Peruvian coke joke on your own? Or did you hear it from someone else?"

"Huh? Wait . . ." Mike immediately looked at the

guy on his right to see if he'd told Donna somehow. The guy quickly shook his head and stepped back, away from the circle.

Donna leaned toward Mike. "What have you ever done with your life? You've never tried anything. You're a fucking piece of shit. And you fucking know it."

Two more men took a step back from that circle as Donna turned to walk down the hall. That familiar hallway smell now standing as a reminder of regret, of trying to retrace her steps as if in some dream where everything gets erased behind you and you can never get back to where you were before. It was that. She had nothing in her foundation anymore. There was a hollowness, and she knew all she had was *now*, and all she was was *her*, and all she knew was that they were wrong.

9

Annabelle. 52.
Entertainment Account Executive.

That face, that look. Another one. Another damn one.

Annabelle was amused still, though so very close to crushing anger.

Even before these women left on their vacation weeks, she knew their plan. Sometimes it was the face, but sometimes the upper arms, or the teeth, or the hair newly bleached. She knew they'd come back to the office with something new, something changed, further away from their real lives and nearer to "the look."

Annabelle didn't know if they all pulled inspiration for "the look" from a single source, an early headshot of one of those game show hostesses perhaps, presenting and stepping around new car after new car, their long blond hair in a silky wave, the teeth whitened, the breasts high and hard, the face ironed and filled and tanned. Or if all these women just wound up looking alike because the procedures all fell in the same direction: the same blond hair tone, the same teeth-whitening solution, the same Botox injection locations, the same fillers, the same "maintenance face-lifts." The more components you took on, the more completely you perfected the look.

For every one year Annabelle worked at this company, she "aged" two. She wasn't doing anything, her photos year to year weren't much different, but her inaction against her actual age made her look older, compared with the other women in the office. Every year Annabelle stayed her age, the other women ironed and bleached and filled away from their age. It wasn't all the women here, there were some too young for that yet. New hires, interns, not yet afraid of things not coming their way, but absorbing it, Annabelle was sure, seeing the panic being modeled for them in that office.

Not even on-camera. None of these women's jobs required them to be on-camera. No. They were the producers, the publicists, the coordinators. None of them were ever on-camera, and yet they all terrified themselves into thinking they should look ready for it. It was an erasure, really. Annabelle had become more herself, more confident of her professional abilities, more committed to her own style, more enamored with her unique looks, the older she got. And she had watched Susan and Gina and Harper and Jenny and Lori and Claire and Kira and Denise and Vivian and Nanette and Jill and Pepper all erase their individuality, whatever had made them different. Their different hair colors (now that odd blond color favored by women everywhere who were going gray), their different facial lines, created by their different life experiences, their different physical developments: looser upper arms, smaller breasts, flatter asses. There was no embrace, just a desperate or rather a matter-of-fact backpedal on their own lives.

Did they look upon Annabelle in horror? Fearful for her that she was just getting closer and closer to some automatic professional and personal rejection, as if Annabelle was running headfirst into professional obscurity and personal isolation? She remembered Lori once standing next to her while a legendary female reporter was up on the big monitor by the conference room. "Oh, I worry about that lack of hair," from Lori. The reporter was 80 and her hair was naturally thin, having weaves installed regularly, they knew. Annabelle was struck that Lori wasn't concerned with the reporter, with how the reporter was dealing with the hair loss, not concerned with the reporter at all. Lori was worried about it happening to herself. At 45, Lori was looking at this famous reporter and seeing not her illustrious career and the strides she'd made for women and news reporting in general, but just seeing some appearance element that Lori was sure would destroy all her own options in life.

Annabelle knew that was what the women in her office were desperate to avoid: any appearance elements that could contribute to rejection. And yet ironically over the years, "older-looking" Annabelle had been promoted twice and recently remarried, all while she watched a number of the other women be fired or passed over for promotions, gone or stuck where they were. Divorced, rejected, broken up with. It didn't matter how they looked; there was no way out of any of that. They'd had other "good" events too. New boyfriends, happy husbands, bigger job offers. The bad and the good. But they always assumed the good events were directly related to the changes they'd made in their appearance. Annabelle had decided it was a sort of compulsive disorder or some kind of superstition. If the start of a new relationship immediately followed Lori's filler injections, then a teeth brightening or a face-lift or an upper arm hanging-skin removal was going to bring on another good event. They were convinced of it. And if the teeth whitening didn't do it, didn't bring on the next good event, then that was the woman's fault. She hadn't done the *right* improvement next; that must have been it.

It was control, wanting a feeling of control. Annabelle supposed she wasn't like that because of the way she'd grown up, never really worried about "good" events outweighing the "bad." Always assuming that everyone gets an even collection of them both by the end. Better to just sail through either of them with an even attitude. She guessed that's what made her such a good negotiator, so calm when faced with an impasse, so impossible to rattle by the opposition. Annabelle saw the women in the office as terrified that they weren't in control. Knowing they weren't in control, and yet wanting to be. It's that knowledge that almost makes you fold your hand at the card table, the knowledge that you can't control anything.

But, ah-ha, there's one last card in the river, one card that you dream will complete your hand, be that third-of-a-kind, finish this full house, fill in this straight flush. That last, unturned card in the river is the option to change *your appearance*. Yes. If you cannot change anything around you, if you know you can't change anything around you, you turn to that last card, the one you are "in control of," the option to change yourself. And if you can convince yourself that all the good events are hinged on changes you make to your look, well then, you've got a card of unknown value, the last one, there in the river, that you can turn over again and again and again and again. There is no end to the number of changes you can perpetrate against yourself. No end to the number of times you can turn that glorious card.

Annabelle became exhausted, there at her desk, thinking about it all, about the effort, both emotional and financial, it took to turn that card over and over again. Annabelle felt exhausted, because she didn't think their appearance changes were actually changing anything at all in their lives, except to introduce some tight cycle of manic hope and panic, over and over.

So, Annabelle turned her mind back to her work and tried to not let this become a crushing anger, tried to keep it at a low simmer. Her, with her small jowls and sunspots and silvering hair, with her crow's feet and thin neck skin and loose upper arms. And she stayed there with her comfort and challenge of improving internally, of growing in confidence and not shrinking from it, of letting the outside magnify that even, by accompanying that confidence. She was never going to grab that unturned card in the river and jump on the cycle of manic hope of completing a "winning hand" at the card table. There had to be someone in this office, Annabelle thought, someone giving a dose of reality here, to the interns, to the new hires, the 20-year-olds, the 30-year-olds. Even to the 40-year-olds, the 50-year-olds. Even. Someone modeling a break from that cycle of panic, someone showing that none of that cutting and dying and filling was ever going to tip the balance of "bad" and "good" events. Someone standing still in the tumult, someone living a life without that fear.

10

Frances. 50. Actress.

They had done it.

Ripped her to pieces.

She knew they would.

The difference was that she'd given it to them, given them a perfect storm of events in visual form, a summary of evidence. Each item alone may not have set it off, but all of them together, all of them at once, yes. Frances had given it to them, and yet she told no one. She had planned on keeping it secret, but to *continue* to keep it a secret, continue to *not* explain herself, to not use that free pass of sympathy, that wasn't planned. Every day that she kept the secret, she was a bit more surprised and a bit more protective of the treasure of the secret.

The long flight, the tragic news, the hours and hours of crying, the sleepless night, her 50 years, the early-morning interview, the morning show lighting. All of it rolled into one large shit cigar of criticism, waiting to be lit.

"Call me when you get to the room." Her boyfriend on the phone, her in the taxi from the airport that night. Talking to him then, talking, nothing wrong.

"Call when you get to the room." Not now, why not now? "Call when you get to the room."

Check in. Up into the hotel room. Call back. "In the room!" Bright, fine, looking forward to starting the avalanche of press that week for her new film.

"Bear and Max are dead."

The flinging of something you want to make not true, of something that was true hours ago, something that was true long before you wanted to make it not true.

The "Are you joking?" The "NO! NO!" The thrashing about on the bed there in the hotel room, unable to push the sorrow out through the small tear duct openings. Unable to give the grief an exit except through the guttural, too-loud-for-a-hotel-room voice and the too-small tear ducts. Thrashing about on the bed. Then hanging up and having no expression except the numb hope of the grief passing, wanting it to wash through fast somehow. Numb and weeping, wishing it would pass and feeling it, both at once. No dinner, cancel dinner, bedtime routine. Lie down for bed.

Her mind wouldn't sleep. It ran through what she knew, what she thought she knew. Both dogs hit by a car. Both dead. That morning, right after she left town, hole in the fence, out in the street. Too many people and too many cars in front of the house when her boyfriend got back, after his long morning run. Too many people right there. He saw them, he saw the trauma, absorbed the trauma.

10 p.m., 11:15 p.m.

Frances's mind wouldn't stop imagining the scene, what she thought was the scene, and the scenes leading up to it. Were they playing, chasing? Escaping? Bear running out and Max following to rescue him? To grab him by the scruff of the neck and bring him back in the yard? Or both dogs gleefully escaping, freedom igniting all their synapses? Saw the car coming and braced for it, or didn't see it coming and the freedom just shutting off, just stopping suddenly in a blast of pain?

12 a.m., 2:30 a.m.

Her mind would not shut down, would not stop replaying a series of events she did not witness, a series of events her mind was insisting on assembling, even though her mind knew she wasn't there, not at all.

5 a.m., 6 a.m.

Frances got up. How could she miss this interview this morning, all of them this week, TV and print press for the biggest film of her career? How could she miss it? Maybe two hours of sleep. Bathroom light, mirror, the eyes were beyond repair. Ice from the wine bucket on the table, on the eyes. Frances tried to make the ice help, knew it wouldn't help. Hours and hours of squeezing sorrow out those tiny tear ducts. Hours and hours of not sleeping— those were the third and fourth events in the perfect storm, after the long flight and the tragic news. The fifth event was her age, 50. So what, big deal, but those five things together, she knew that if she went on-camera, on that morning show, she would look the worst she's ever publicly looked.

Put the eye makeup on anyway, going anyway, never a question. Trying not to cry now, the sorrow still there, waiting in a line, a stream, to escape out her tear ducts and out her mouth. Hold it until after, try her hardest. Don't ruin the eye makeup, don't increase the puffiness. Put on the prepared outfit.

Her Planned Joy not finding room on stage now, her Planned Joy confused now and rechecking the script for today, for this entire week of press, the week where the Planned Joy was going to be up front, unmistakably in the spotlight. Grief was there now instead, too large to get off stage, too overwhelming to replace. Could only mollify it for spans of time, could only shove white rags into its mouth and eyes and ears and nostrils to shut it up, to stop the stream, the escape. For short spans of time. The Planned Joy had to stand to the side and not on stage, the casting change too sudden to have been noted in the theater program.

Reckless, damning, unforgivable to go on-camera like this, Frances knew. And she wanted a reckless feeling right now, for it to be that white rag shoved in Grief's mouth, so she could do the press, get through the interviews. "The worst she's ever looked." She knew they'd say that. Was that different than what they'd already said about her face in the past, when her appearance was not soaked with grief? When she looked happy and fine? They had said it then, and they would say it now.

Get out of the cab, at the TV network studio. People to face, make it about the film, promoting the film, promoting the film. The film studio publicist there, the morning show producer there, two security guards. Escorting. Up the elevator. Keep the white rag in, say nothing. Out onto the upper floor, where the studio is, where the morning show is shot. Stop in the makeup room. Maybe, Frances wanted to see. "Maybe here? Can you do something here?" Frances pointed to the swollen, tear-soaked bags under her eyes. The makeup artist then coating a brush with concealer, light-beige cream meant to paint over reality. Strife, fear, annoyance, jealousy, rage, insecurity, worry, GRIEF. Meant to paint over that, cover it, hide it from the public. Hide it so the public can keep thinking that there exists a group of people who have no strife, fear, annoyance, jealousy, rage, insecurity, worry, or grief. That the evidence we look for, that we find, that we've always found in each other's faces, the evidence that has been paramount in our evolutionary survival, to read a face, to know what we are contending with, to know if you're friend or foe, to know what we are walking into. Cover that. Make the public think that they themselves are diseased somehow, because their strife, fear, annoy-

ance, jealousy, rage, insecurity, worry, or grief does
show on their faces, that they continue to telegraph
these things, continue to expel information through
their faces, that they're not like this group, this covered group, the ones who always have a poker face
of success and happiness and satisfaction and ease
and financial security.

"Never mind, it's OK," Frances to the makeup
artist. Frances wanted to keep the recklessness,
and she knew the beige concealer wouldn't pull that
Grief off stage anyway. She knew she'd just look
like someone who had cried all night and not slept
and was 50 and here at 7 a.m. (the sixth element in
this perfect storm), but then had put concealer under her eyes. It wouldn't erase the dog-death grief.
It wouldn't change the situation and she didn't want
any of those who had criticized her face before to
think she was thinking of them, thinking of them and
what they might say and painting concealer under
her eyes to satisfy them, in hopes they would be
pleased that she was trying to look like someone
who never shows strife, fear, annoyance, jealousy,
rage, insecurity, worry, or grief on her face.

Frances then stood off-camera, waiting for her
introduction, to go on the set and sit before the
morning show host and the gaggle of morning show
audience members, brightly dressed in solid colors
of rapt engagement. Frances waited to disappoint
them, after the wildly enthusiastic and flattering in-

troduction, to step on stage, dripping with sorrow. White rag in Grief's mouth and ears and nostrils, yes, but falling out a bit from the eyes. Grief not completely mollified right now. Keep it together. The face.

Frances knew that she might as well have been walking on the set, before the cameras, topless, wearing a diaper, with shit smeared over her limbs. Walking on stage with this face, puffy with grief—it was reckless. Frances knew, now walking onto the set and shaking the morning show host's hand and sitting in the assigned chair under burning, bright, overhead lights (the last element of this perfect storm) with this face, to not have canceled this appearance instead, was a violent affront to society. To the millions of people watching this at home, drinking coffee, making the kids' lunches, folding laundry, leaving for work; to the brightly dressed studio audience, to the host, to the crew there, to the film studio publicist watching from the wings. Everyone. Outrageous behavior from Frances. Outrageous. Irresponsible.

Talking about the film, the character, to the morning show host. Frances knew she could change this narrative right there. Change it from "The worst she's ever looked" to "Oh, that poor dear." One sentence. That's all she needed. One: "My dogs were killed yesterday." To pause from talking about the film, take a moment, maybe let Grief release one tear out of the left tear duct, and then say it. One sentence. She knew it, almost did it. At the 30-second mark of the interview, there, almost. But that would have been for those who had criticized her face. Just for them. That would have been Frances putting aside the film, everyone who had worked on it, the film studio, her excitement for her role, everything aside to make an appeal to those who have criticized her face in the past, the ones she knew were lining up to criticize her right now, in real time, on message boards, on social media right now, live-tweeting, as the morning show was airing. Frances didn't want to say the one sentence, to fold under the shelter of pity, so she didn't. She wanted to keep the focus on the film and not let her week of press be polluted, overwhelmed, by the dead-dog grief, to not let Grief take a larger stage, with larger orifices into which to shove white, mollifying rags, to not let "Oh, that poor dear" interfere with not only this week of film press, but to also become a footnote in all Frances's future press. "That time, years ago, she bravely promoted her film, right after the deaths, in spite of the tragic news. Oh, that poor dear."

No. And that pathetic, sniveling sympathy, that interference with her press week, that lingering dead-dog pity, would be for what? So Frances could desperately pander to people who had cruelly, aggressively, maliciously criticized her face in the past? No. She wasn't going to do it. She kept the secret through the interview, with her face of grief, puffy eyes, sorrowful countenance, verge of tears, 50 years old, 7 a.m., blaring, overhead, morning-show lights. And she kept the secret the next day and the next day, in front of more cameras, giving more interviews, Grief getting smaller on-stage, the white-rag-stuffing becoming less needed, until she was done.

And they came.

They did it.

They ripped her to pieces.

On social media, on blogs, in media "think pieces."

Just like she knew they would.

11

Tara. 42. Photographer.

Gloria looked pretty. Different? Just happy? Tara couldn't tell. Pretty, anyway.

"God, a year? Has it been a year since I saw you last?"

"Two."

"Oh wow. Two years."

Tara and Gloria opened their menus.

"The soups are really good here, if you're in the mood." Gloria was a bit older, not much, but older. Had "gone before" Tara in ways, over the years. Married before Tara, had kids before Tara, got divorced before Tara. Someone Tara could call for advice or tips on what was coming next.

"Salad's good for me."

The waiter was there.

"The spinach salad."

"I'll have the tomato soup," from Gloria.

The waiter moved off.

Gloria leaned in. "How is everything? What's going on?"

"Everything's good really. The kids are fine. They

adjusted way better than I thought they would after the divorce."

"Well, they're so young. It's easier if they're young. They don't know anything else."

"Yeah, maybe. Dan wanted to 'have dinner' the other night. I don't know what that was supposed to mean. I just said it wasn't a good time. I mean, c'mon. Let's be divorced for a year before we try to be best friends or whatever."

"Yeah, that happens. It's pretty common."

Tara was annoyed at Gloria already. She loved her, looked up to her even, but always with the fucking advice or counsel or whatever Gloria thought she was supposed to shovel into this friendship. Annoying, is all.

Tara changed the subject. "What about *you*? You were traveling, right? Africa? Is that right?"

"Yeah! Africa. God, I haven't seen you in a long time. That was last year. We have this new guided tour that goes down these fantastic rivers. Did one in Portugal recently and another one in China."

"Wow. You got pictures?"

Gloria took out her phone. "You should come out on one of these tours. Bring the kids. Seriously, I can get you a discount through my employee rate." She turned her phone to Tara. "I love this one. This boat tour was at Three Gorges in China. Look at the waterfalls."

"Amazing."

The waiter put the salad and the soup on the table.

Gloria dipped her spoon into the soup. "Can you tell?"

"Can I tell?"

"I had a mini-lift."

Tara felt her stomach sink slightly. "Really?" She tried to say it brightly. She tried to not let the disappointment tinge her voice.

"Yeah, look." Gloria turned to the right and to the left. "Remember how I was getting those big folds at the side of my mouth? And how my eyes were getting a bit hooded? I had just the smallest lift and it made a big difference. I mean, it just looks better, right? Like you can hardly tell about the lift, but it all just looks better."

"You look really pretty!" Tara was crushed. Crushed.

"Thanks."

"You looked good before, though," Tara said carefully.

"Aw, thanks. But, you'll see. A little maintenance goes a long way."

Tara smiled politely. "I guess."

"You're not there yet, not quite. I can give you her name when you're ready."

Tara suddenly felt infuriated. Infuriated that Gloria had succumbed and did this to her face, infuriated that Gloria was now matter-of-factly telling Tara that it was something she should do soon.

"Oh, that's OK." Tara smiled tightly, tried to stay calm.

Gloria put her spoon down. "Here, I'll text you her contact info."

Tara stared for a moment. "Uh, that's OK . . . Thanks, that's OK." She forked some spinach and goat cheese.

"Oh, I just sent it." Gloria put the phone down and started buttering some bread. "Do a consultation, at least. Dr. Robinson is the best. She'll tell you what you need."

"I don't . . . Gloria, please. I'm not in the market . . ."

"I get it, I get it. Just go and talk to her. Maybe not this week. Maybe next week."

Tara set her fork down and put her hand on the napkin in her lap. "Gloria, I don't want to do it . . . It's not for me, OK?"

Gloria had a slightly shocked look on her face now. She put the buttered bread down. "OK. Sure. No big deal."

"Look, I'm not wanting to . . . offend. It's just not for me."

"I get it. I get it," she said quickly.

Tara was amazed that Gloria had now spun this exchange to put herself in the victim seat.

"I'm just looking out for you," Gloria added.

". . . Oh my God," from Tara. Politeness slipping.

Silence. Forks on china. Muddled conversations at other tables.

Gloria smiled. "Are we having a bad lunch now?" Then, conceding: "Hey, I'm sorry. OK? I didn't mean . . ."

"It's OK."

"I get it. It's not for everyone."

"OK," Tara said tersely.

"Hey, so tell me more about Dan's 'let's have dinner' request."

Tara smiled slightly. "Yeah . . . like I said, I don't know what his goal is there. Anyway. I'm more focused on doing some dating now, so I don't have time to start some dinner thing with him."

"Dating! Great. Any good candidates?"

"Ah, not sure yet. We'll see."

The waiter again. "Coffee, ladies? Desserts?"

"I'll have a coffee."

"Me too."

Tara looked at Gloria. She knew she couldn't be friends with her anymore. "Why didn't you just deal?"

"Huh?"

"Why didn't you just deal with it?"

"What? Deal with what?"

"Whatever. Your . . . insecurity or feeling old or wanting to . . . look young, I don't know. Why didn't you just deal with it?"

Gloria's face hardened a bit suddenly. "You think I didn't deal with things? That's exactly what I did."

"God, Gloria," Tara said softly, "why didn't you just deal with the insecurity instead of cutting your face?"

Silence.

"Hmm . . . I think maybe we should go."

"I'm not trying to insult you. I just want to know why you forfeited an opportunity to grow as a person. I mean, every dissatisfaction we have with ourselves is an opportunity to like ourselves more than what other people think, right?" Tara said, hopefully.

Gloria was looking for the waiter now. "I think maybe you don't know what you're talking about."

Tara dropped the politeness completely now. "Shit . . . I get it. We're not going to be friends after this . . . But, I just want to let you know that I *do* know what I'm talking about. And I think you have started down a road you're not going to be able to get off of. And it's not just going to be a bunch of procedures and the money you'll spend . . ."

The coffee on the table.

"Can we get the check?" flatly, from Gloria to the waiter.

Tara continued, sadly, as if she were holding Gloria's wrists off the side of a boat, in the middle of the night, and Gloria was making no effort to get back into the boat. "But, just, you're giving up chances to not give a shit about other people's comments. To just go beyond that."

Gloria put some cash down on the table and stood up. "Tara, thanks for advice. I didn't ask for it. I'm glad everything is going well for you. I'm going to get back to my life."

Tara stood up. "Hey, I've been taking your unsolicited advice for years. I think you should just listen to this one thing. I always thought you were pretty incredible, and then you go and do this and it makes me feel like it was all a lie. That you were this adventurous, independent woman and now you're just doing the opposite. You're people-pleasing the group that cares the *least* about you. I wish you saw that."

"Well, I can see that *you* don't care much about me." Gloria started to move past her.

Tara turned, blocking her path. "You're never going to go anywhere like this. You're never going to know yourself."

Gloria looked at her. "Can you get out of the fucking way?"

Gloria walked on, out the door, to her car. Tara sat back down at the table. Strangely, she felt happier than she'd felt in a long time. She'd said those things for Gloria's benefit, but saying those things had also pushed Tara into an area of resolve she hadn't yet known. An area where she committed to take every insecure feeling about getting older and spin it into confidence gold. Instead of cutting her face, she was going to get to the other side. She was not going to throw the opportunities aside and allow the waves of criticism to pull her down to the sandy bottom. Instead, she was going to swim out farther and get stronger for it. That was what she was going to do.

12

Cara. 40. Housewife.

Cara at the hair salon.
"Succeeding"
The more Cara looks like she is a success, the more she separates herself from those who are not succeeding. Those who are not succeeding are bogged down with struggle and disappointment and things like that. And you can see that by looking at them. The key is to *not* look like them.

Cara at pilates class.
"Triumphing"
Keeping one's physical appearance as polished and fresh as possible is an easily recognized method of demonstrating this separation from those who are suffering and not succeeding.

Cara at a Botox party, getting a touch-up.
"Winning"
The more Cara looks as if she's winning, the more Cara will attract winning situations, and live in happiness and satisfaction.

Cara picking up her tailored silk trousers.
"Dominating"
Cara consulting with Judy's plastic surgeon.
"Flourishing"
It's the manifestation of the American Dream. If you can look it, you can have it. Good things come to those who look like winners and Cara is taking the proper steps.

Cara getting a hot stone massage.
"Overcoming"
Cara on the telephone, hearing that her mother is ill.
"Sobbing"
If Cara looks like she's suffering or weary or sad, she will not look like someone who attracts success. And then happiness may not come her way. Cara must work at overcoming any visible indication of the undesirable parts of life, like sadness.

Cara getting an acid peel.
"Thriving"
Cara fighting with her husband.
"Draining"
Cara must be diligent to erase any visible proof of irritation, exhaustion, frustration, disappointment, or hopelessness. She must take whatever steps are necessary.

Cara getting fillers injected into her face.

"Prospering"
Cara being flipped off by her teenage daughter.
"Angering"
Cara must delete the parts of her that repel success and happiness, like stress, annoyance, and displeasure. More importantly, Cara must remove any physical evidence that would indicate to others that she is not free of unwelcome elements like disappointment and worry.

Cara being prepped for facial surgery.
"Erasing"

Cara's face being cut open and trimmed and stretched and sewn.
"Deleting"

Cara recovering, swollen and black and blue.
"Eradicating"
Cara has a true American Spirit. She's willing to do whatever it takes to increase the separation of her as someone who can attract success and happiness, from anything (or anybody) that would repel that success and happiness.

Now, Cara's mother later dying and her husband divorcing her and her daughter refusing to speak to her may be an indication that Cara needs to more perfectly look like someone who attracts success and happiness, someone lacking any evidence of the rigors of life.

We've got faith in Cara! She's a dedicated devotee of perfection. We know she'll take the time, and spend the money, to continuously improve her physical appearance in order to someday live a happy life.

13

Virginia. 54. Actress.

"Why don't I feel right?"

Virginia sat in the back of the black town car she'd called to take her to the red carpet event. The driver was taking the long way, but Virginia didn't say anything. It was better for her to get to the event a little late, even if the delay left her alone with her thoughts beyond what was comfortable.

"Why do I feel off-balance?"

Virginia shifted in her seat and looked out the window in an effort to settle her confidence. The closed and darkened window reflected her face. Virginia looked more closely at her reflection. There was a crease. It seemed new. She took off her sunglasses and looked again.

The driver made a left turn and the light shifted. The window now not so completely a mirror. Virginia pawed at her clutch purse for her compact mirror. She looked into it and felt her stomach tighten. She breathed in and out carefully. She knew she could fix it. It was at the side of the mouth, on the right. Maybe the fillers had begun to shrink, or maybe it was time to finally do the slight pull her plastic surgeon had mentioned.

"It's OK," she said out loud, under her breath.
"It's OK."

Was that it? The uneasiness she felt today. Was it
the crease? She must have registered it earlier today,
seen the crease out of the corner of her eye, but not
consciously registered it. The awareness must have
been gently festering in her head, and was only now
making itself known.

Virginia made a note in her phone to schedule an
appointment with Dr. Freed after the event. The cameras would be at the red carpet drop-off. The crease
would be fine. She knew how to hold her head so
that the maximum amount of flash would fill that spot
in. Soon it would be fixed and she wouldn't have to
accommodate it.

The "fixing" had done that each time, taken the
burden off Virginia to accommodate these flaws as
her career progressed. First it was the breast implants
so she could continue to do the suggestive scenes
for which she was known. Then it was the upper arm
reduction to maintain those sinewy "dancer's arms."
Next was the face: some fillers, the under-eye bag
removal, some Botox. And, of course, the removal
of the loose skin around the knees, so Virginia could
maintain that "best legs in the business" title and her
trademark miniskirt look. All small changes, imper-
ceptible, perhaps. She could then keep the bedroom
scenes, the tank tops, the side-lit close-ups, the
miniskirts. She didn't have to change; she could be

the same. The same Virginia Klauss, internationally known film star, still "She looks amazing" and "How does she do it?" and "She never ages."

That was the thing to work at, the looks. After all, it was just about the only thing the public noticed. The more they aged and she didn't, the more they worshipped her. Her constant look made her seem otherwordly, even godlike. Sure, her roles were less frequent, but Virginia rationalized that it was because she was choosy. She didn't have to take all those "mom" roles other actresses her age took. She could hold out for roles that were better suited to the kind of actress she'd always been.

Virginia smiled at the thought. While her contemporaries took more character roles, and even roles dealing with the physical and mental challenges of getting older, Virginia resisted. So, less roles, and even a move to a smaller talent agency, when her larger agency felt she wasn't working enough. Sure, the larger agency had more prestige and power, but the smaller one understood the image she wanted to maintain. After all, every fix Virginia went through had great potential to jump-start her career. Every time she "freshened up" her look, there was a great possibility that someone would take notice and cast her more frequently in the ingénue-type roles for which she was known.

Virginia was always the prettiest one in the room and she was going to do whatever it took to maintain that position. Thankfully, she'd had sons and not daughters, so there'd be no comparison of herself to some younger version of her. No, she'd escaped that fate. So, she would fix this new crease. It wasn't a big deal. Maybe a mini-lift, not a big deal. She couldn't get comfortable, though. It was cold in the car? It was taking too long to get to the event?

"Do you think you even look like *you* anymore?" Her youngest son, last time she'd seen him. He'd always been the rude one, she thought. His "death by a thousand cuts" reference to her face, her body, her look. So rude. Virginia tried to shake the memory off, but it was pushing that uneasy feeling open. The feeling she already had, it was pushing it open.

"How close are we?" she suddenly asked the driver.

"There was some road closure, a marathon or something—"

"Sure. How close are we?"

The driver mumbled some time length. There wasn't a number that was going to put Virginia at ease. She had to collect herself, but didn't exactly know how. She felt off-balance. Yes, definitely. She closed her eyes and tried to breathe again. In and out. She clasped her leather clutch bag tighter, tried to remind herself that, with the exception of the new crease by the side of her mouth, everything was perfect. The legs, the clothes, the arms, the breasts, the face, the hair. Everything had been critically looked over and fixed. But, some door had been opened just a bit, some knob had been turned and some door had been gently pushed ajar.

She was 54. No surgery was going to change that. What if those ingénue roles never came back? What if they continued to give them to 20- and 30-year-olds? Virginia took her phone out again and googled herself, looked at her pictures online. Back and forth between her 20-year-old self and her 54-year-old self. She looked just the same. The same.

Virginia sat back in the seat more relaxed. Less acting work, her youngest son (and maybe the middle one as well) upset with her. It was OK. So long as she looked the same, she felt in control. And in a business where one has little control, where an actress is subject to casting directors' whims, to studio executives' whims, to the public's whims, Virginia knew that feeling of control was important. Even if it was as a beetle stuck in amber, even if it was as an Egyptian mummy in a sarcophagus of appearance fixing, even then, Virginia felt like she was in control.

14

Rosemary. 56. Wife.

She loved the lights in her walk-in closet, even though she didn't need that flattering, eye-level, warm-bulb lighting, really. Rosemary had done the right things. Small adjustments in her early 40s, face-lift at 52: she'd done the right things. She didn't need that lighting, not like some others did.

"That wasn't too bad. Right?" Her husband, throwing his linen button-up shirt in the corner of the closet, just a foot from the hamper. "Brad's wife was OK, right?" He pulled her hair back from her face and kissed her. "Brad's a big client, so that's great that you two were talking."

As Steven moved to the bed, she could see him in the closet mirrors, behind her. She hung up her black silk dress, peeled off her stockings, and threw them into the trash by her sweater shelves. "She was perfectly fine. People should give her a chance."

He had already burrowed himself under the duvet. "She's just new. They're just new to town. They'll settle in." His voice was muffled by the camel-colored cashmere throw blanket up near his chin.

Rosemary took off her jade and platinum earrings

and her thin gold bracelets, dropped them on her dressing table in the closet, and pulled a chiffon tank top off a padded hanger.

"You should give her your plastic surgeon's number." Steven's voice was already relaxed, under the mound of soft bedding.

The chiffon brushed Rosemary's cheeks as she pulled the tank top over her head. "I didn't want to say anything yet. It was only the second time we'd met."

"Well, Brad's going to need to do that."

"Yeah, obviously." She slipped her legs under the bedcovers and sat there, looking at the jar of caviar face cream on the bedside table.

"It'll help her fit in too."

Rosemary unscrewed the jar and started smoothing the cream onto her face. "He can't be representing that company, and driving a Maserati, and then not fix his wife's face."

"Yeah . . . It just makes it look like they're not paying him enough. He'll have to get that done."

"Am I rubbed in?" Rosemary's face hovered over Steven's, her eyes closed.

Steven opened one eye, just a slit. "Yeah."

Rosemary turned off her Venetian glass bedside lamp and erased her body under the feather-filled covers.

"It would really be a bad reflection on Brad, and on that company, really, if she didn't get a face-lift.

I mean, I don't know her that well; what if she re-fused? He might as well be driving a beat-up station wagon to meetings. It will really be a bad reflection, could affect his deals, you know, people assuming he doesn't have the money."

"He'll do it. Don't worry." Steven's eyes were closed.

"She could make it look like the company *itself* isn't doing well. God, they should have gotten it done before he moved out here, really. Then again, I'm sure Dr. Rouss will do a better job with her face here than someone would have in London."

"Rose, c'mon. I gotta be up at five."

Rosemary's face was heavy now on her laven-der satin pillow. "Jeannie calls it *status-ignorant,* and she's right. There's no excuse for it."

"Brad'll fix it," Steven mumbled.

Rosemary closed her eyes and listened to her heart beat fast in her ears, on the pillow. It sounded like a tiny person taking quick steps in the snow. Crunch, crunch, crunch, crunch, crunch. This whole business was embarrassing for Brad and his wife. What kind of man lets his wife walk around like that? But, Brad would fix it, she told herself, as she fell asleep. Brad would fix it.

15

Billie. 49. Real Estate Agent.

Billie resented Karen. Of course she did.

Karen, porcelain-smooth skin, plump lips spreading over stark white teeth, handing out cupcakes in exchange for the middle school kids' grimy dollar bills. Smiling, flashing teeth, tossing brass hair. Ripe bosom threatening to splash from the low neck of her cashmere sweater. Leaning over the bake sale table and standing up, leaning over and standing up. Billie imagined the children would welcome Karen's full, naked breasts as a righteous reminder of all that was life-sustaining and necessary. The faculty and nearby parents would also greet these bare, gravity-defying, lilac-scented mounds as a sign from God that all is right in the world and that goodness prevails. A rainbow after the rain. That's what Billie imagined would happen if Karen's goddamn fake tits fell out of her slutty-neck sweater right now.

Billie put her platter of Valentine's brownies on the bake sale table near Karen and pulled the cellophane off. A pastel-colored candy heart was pressed into the top of each gooey square. *HUBBA HUBBA, KISS ME, LOVE YOU, YOU ROCK* dotted the darkness. Karen suddenly turned to Billie. Her breasts, her face, her hair. Big smile. Big smile.

"Hi, Billie!" Big hug. "How are you?! We're here at the same time this year? I feel like we never have the same volunteer times!"

Billie focused on not letting her grin slip, on not letting her face telegraph her incredulity at the undisturbed surface of Karen's face. The absence of pores, creases, age spots, or sagging. It was smooth, as if a mask had been made from the skin of a baby and transplanted onto Karen.

"Oh, I think I'm relieving you. My time starts at 2."

Karen looked at her watch and Billie resented her for wearing one, and not just checking her phone for the time, like everyone else. "Oh right! I didn't notice what time it was. Wow, that just flew by!" Big smile, milk-white teeth.

Billie carefully let her grin grow. "Yeah, I guess!"

A teacher tapped Karen on the shoulder and Karen turned to direct her enthusiasm at him instead. Billie looked at the back of Karen's head for a moment. She wanted to ask her about her face. She wanted to ask her about before the first time, before the procedures piled up and became too hard for Billie to keep track of, if before the first time, if Karen was worried at all about what could happen. Worried that it would go terribly wrong. That she'd look in the mirror afterward at awkwardly stretched cheeks, a glossy forehead, and comically swollen lips, and regret it all. Did

Karen worry that she'd wind up sobbing on her kitchen floor, making bargains with God to go back in time and reverse the surgery, swear on her children's lives that she'd never be ungrateful for her face again, never complain about the bags or the jowls, or the thin lips or the heavy eyelids? Billie wanted to ask Karen if she ever had a moment of terror like that. Or even a moment of concern that others would afterward not take her seriously, that they would be stuck in the Uncanny Valley of buoyant breasts, a velvety face, and golden hair on the frame of a 50-year-old woman.

Billie instead looked down at her brownies and turned them with the hearts' text facing the student customers across the table. She knew she could never have plastic surgery. She'd be too worried of something going wrong, of looking worse than before. Even if the surgery was a success, she'd feel like she was lying to everyone she encountered and would have to watch them silently accept the lie of an unlined face, as if she were a retarded child wearing a Halloween costume every day that the townspeople politely accommodate by not mentioning it.

"Yes, a dollar apiece." Billie took three dollars from the girls and pushed the money into the wide slit of the metal cashbox.

The girls giggled and grabbed the *KISS ME, NO WAY*, and *ASK ME* brownies.

"Here you go." Billie held out some napkins imprinted with pink hearts. The girls grinned and one shook her head no.

Karen was farther away now. Billie could see her near the drink stand by the gym door, talking to another parent. Karen was laughing at something the other woman said, and placed a manicured hand briefly on her shoulder. Billie wanted to punch Karen in the mouth.

Billie had been wronged, she felt cheated. Billie had been beautiful, was still beautiful to some. But Karen did not grow up beautiful, was not beautiful as a child, not as a teen, and not as a young adult, Billie knew this. Karen had been average, a 7, Billie knew. Billie, on the other hand, had been a 10, considered a 10, for years. As Billie aged, though, she felt like her ranking fell. 9, 8, 7, 6. And all things being equal, Karen's 7 of years past should be a 3 right now, by Billie's account. A fucking 3. But Karen cheated. That's what pissed Billie off. Karen fucking cheated. Breast implants, face-lift, teeth whitening, hair bleaching. Karen fucking hit the nitro button on her car and passed Billie. Fucking cheated. "Karen looks amazing for her age," and all that bullshit. Fucking fake-ass 3, posing as a 7.

"I better get out of here before I start eating the merchandise!" Karen was next to Billie now at the table, pulling her apron over her head, and laughing at her own joke. Billie smiled and nodded. Karen handed her the apron. "You want this?" The stiff red cotton was choked in Karen's fist, behind her pale-pink, heart-charmed nails.

Billie looked at the nails for a moment, and wanted to break half of them off.

She looked up at Karen. "Sure."

Karen fluffed her hair and exhaled loudly. "OK!" She reached for her purse under the bake sale table. "Billie, you should come along next time we have a mom's night out! I'm chairing that committee now, so I get to pick the bar." Karen winked, or she seemed to wink. She was moving away now, pawing through her bag in search of her car keys. "Let me know where you want to go! The next one's in March!" Karen then looked up at Billie, smiled widely, and waved with the entirety of her arm.

"Fuck you, Karen," Billie said under her breath as she smiled a smile to match Karen's, and waved back just as big.

16

Bella. 46. Actress.

The dressing room trailer door opened suddenly.

It was dark in the trailer. The early-morning light fell heavily through the open door and split the darkness where Bella sat before the small table and mirror.

She jerked her hand up, blocking the light from her eyes.

"Oh! Bella, I'm so sorry. I thought you had left already."

Bella's eyes wouldn't adjust to the light. "It's OK, Heather. You can come in."

Heather held up a bottle of toner and a package of cotton balls. "I just brought these over from the makeup trailer. I didn't know if you had run out."

Bella gestured for her to enter. "Thanks."

Heather stepped up into the small dressing room. Bella still had her character's wardrobe on. Heather put the toner and cotton ball bag on the table. "I thought you left the second we wrapped . . . Night shoots are the worst. I hate heading home to sleep while everyone else is just starting their day and driving to work."

Bella looked up and smiled a bit. Her eyes were swollen from crying. "Oh, yeah. That's true."

Heather stood there for a moment. "Do you want me to clean your face? I know it was really dusty in there."

Bella nodded gently and turned back to the mirror. Heather squeezed some toner onto a cotton ball, and the smell of roses drifted into the trailer. She passed the cotton ball over Bella's forehead, back and forth quietly. She tossed the darkened cotton into the trash next to Bella's leg. Heather soaked another one with more rose toner and wiped Bella's skin from her temple to her jaw.

Bella looked somewhere on the table. "You're not supposed to see dailies. The actors. I mean, some do, but . . . you're not supposed to."

"Oh. Did you watch the dailies from our film?" Another browned cotton ball into the trash.

"I shouldn't have done that. They invited me, though. And I've been doing this for a long time . . . It shouldn't have . . . It's a performance, a character . . ." Bella's voice caught in her throat.

Heather stared at her and then put her hand on Bella's shoulder for just a moment before moistening another cotton ball. "Did it . . . You didn't like the scenes you saw?"

"I was really excited about taking this role. They don't usually let me play roles like this, you know? I was 'the perfect girl' part for so long. When I was in my 20s. You think they can't get past that . . . and then you get a part like this. It's great . . . No makeup, really raw, you know."

"Really great." Heather ran the cotton ball along Bella's neck.

"When I see myself in the mirror, I think, 'I look pretty good.' Maybe I don't see as sharply as the camera with my eyes now, but the dailies just . . . You see every tiny thing."

"You look beautiful."

"I've done Botox before and done fillers and I can't even . . . I mean, I try to do the minimum amount so I don't distort the way I look, but I don't even want to do that. I so want to be able to just be . . ." Bella trailed off.

"Was it the scene by the bridge? That was a really great scene."

Bella smiled a little.

Silence.

"Yeah, that was one of them. When I did the scene, I knew I was hitting it right for the character. You know, she's really struggling there, really reaching the end of her ability to hold onto reality. I know . . . I really nailed it."

"Well, that's terrific, right?" Heather chirped, a little too loud, a little too bright.

Bella turned in her metal folding chair, away from the mirror, and faced the door. "I didn't want it," she said softly.

"Pardon?" Heather bent down to hear Bella better, see Bella better.

Bella looked up at Heather suddenly. "Sorry. You have to get going, I know . . ." She stood. "I should change, so wardrobe can take this outfit out of here. I'm sorry."

Heather moved back to the table and started screwing the top on the rose toner bottle. "From what I've seen, your work is really good here. I'd never seen you play a character like this . . . This is the kind of role that gets awards."

Bella covered her face with her hands. "I know." A tear drifted through the fingers on one hand.

"Bella, what's the matter?" Again trying to save the moment with the tone of her voice. Heather's hopeful cheerfulness trying to convert Bella's emotions.

"It all felt so right and it's there on the screen. It's right, it's good . . . But, I just . . . I don't want it. I look tired and old, and not valuable. Even though what I was bringing to it emotionally was much more real and much more fulfilling from a performance standpoint, but visually . . . I look so bad. There's the lighting, I know, but . . . They're going to say, 'Oh, she looks old and tired . . .' and not hire me again. My whole career has been 'Oh, she's so pretty! Oh, she's so hot!' and now they'll say, 'But now she's a middle-aged woman, and this is how she looks.' It's vanity, I know. It's vanity . . ."

Heather offered her a tissue and a crooked smile.

Bella took the tissue and stood there for a moment. "I thought they would finally *see me,* that now that I'm doing this kind of role, they would see past my looks and see the performance . . . But I think they're still just going to notice my looks and nothing else. Beautiful or ugly, that's all they want to see."

Heather shifted her weight slowly to her other hip. Heather, the makeup artist, an agent of artifice. She didn't want any of this to be true. She didn't want Bella to be concerned, to be affected, to be crushed by others' superficiality. She didn't want it to be true that the loudest audience members were the ones most offended by an older actress's face. She didn't want it to be true.

But, she knew what was out there. Not yet feeling it herself, at just 34, but knowing it was out there. Actresses worshipped as beautiful when young, growing older and seeing the pretty façade from their 20s, the one they felt was distracting audiences from really seeing them, slipping to the floor. And now instead of the audience clearly seeing them there, absent of the façade, everyone is instead staring at the floor, where the façade lies. They are busy mourning the death of that beautiful veneer that they valued above all else.

17

Jade. 43. Wife.

"Do you love me?"

"You know I do."

On the boat, the yacht. Jade called it the boat. Off the coast of southern France. For the third time; she thought it was the third time. Yes, once for her 23rd birthday, once for their 10th anniversary, and now. The third time.

A glass of champagne in each hand, Luc nuzzled her neck on his way out to the deck. "What's Jacques making for lunch?"

She reached back for him from the velvet couch, as he moved past her. "Lobster soup and some avocado something. I set the menus so long ago . . ."

"Great."

Jade turned and draped her bronzed arms over the back of the couch to watch Luc hand the champagne to their guests. A young woman, younger than Jade, a personal chef or an illustrator, Jade couldn't remember. Susie? Shelly? Demetri, one of Luc's business partners, older and attractively relaxed, like aged European men can so often be. Another woman, a friend of the business partner, younger again than

Jade, but older than the personal chef, and decidedly more blasé to be on the boat. There were others, sort of smudges of people. Jade couldn't remember if she'd met them before on their travels. Maybe.

Squinting at the sunny deck, Jade put on her black sunglasses and heaved herself off the couch to join them.

"Jade!" and "Have you cooled off now?" and "Lunch is served!" Jacques was waving everyone over to the long table on the deck. Lavender overflowed the two vases on the white tablecloth. Lobster bisque and avocado salad at every place setting. Luc helped Susie/Shelly into a deck chair next to himself and Jade sat between the Blasé Woman and Demetri. Jade looked at Luc and marveled at the length of their marriage. Married him so young, her 22 to his 42. Funny to have been married for the same amount of years as their age difference.

Jade smiled and talked with Demetri, about his ski chalet in Portillo, Chile. "Use it, please, I'm never there." The Blasé Woman dipped her spoon into the soup, perhaps as a gesture of cooperation, and then quickly asked for more champagne. Luc was laughing at something Susie/Shelly said. Jade smiled. Susie/Shelly seemed nice. Perhaps she'd cook them a meal or two when they returned home to Berlin. Luc could fly her out.

Full now. Just the soup and the salad, but the rich flavors creating a satisfying wholeness inside Jade.

Relaxing. She just felt relaxed. Had brought a few books. Hadn't been reading much recently, but this seemed like a good trip to bring them on. She'd been right. She had read two already; three more books left. The light in the sky was just starting to turn to that rich, honeyed late-afternoon sunlight. The water glittered around the boat.

The rest of the trip happened in patches. A few more days, it might have been two weeks, Jade didn't know how much that mattered. It was a collapsing of time. It happened all at once, but spread out, like torture. Catching them, but not catching them. No dramatic discovery of an embrace, her husband and Susie/Shelly, of a pressing together, naked and salty from a swim. Not that. It was more of an in-evitable tumbling. Puzzle pieces that meant nothing on their own, but too many of them, close to each other, making an impossible-to-now-erase picture. An ah-ha moment, the certainty, the inevitability of Luc and Susie/Shelly. Jade hadn't known, but could not now relate to the Jade who didn't know. So obvious now, so glaring.

Undulating on the sea, days or weeks more, Jade couldn't tell, couldn't recall, until they were back to shore, until Jade could be physically apart from this new Luc, Luc with Susie/Shelly. There were reasons. She heard reasons. After the numbness and the tears. No hysteria, she wasn't sure why. No anger, just sadness. The reasons made sense to Luc, but not to Jade. They made sense to Luc, of course. It was what she'd heard about. Woman married to a man, a life, a city, a house, a social world. All one, all in the one package. She'd known some women, mostly back in Los Angeles and New York, who had desperately tried to ensure the continued inclusion in their own lives, the lives that seemingly hung on the husband's acceptance or rejection. A whole world. Jade had felt exempt from that. She'd been sure that she and Luc shared something deeper. She'd felt exempt from the chasing of a smooth, unlined face. That was how it manifested, this insurance. Unmarked, fastidiously kept, a face. Many of her friends had panicked at their looser necks, the creases near the eyes. Not old enough, many of them, to really display the typical signposts of age, but any hint of it, any indication of the possibility that they could look older and incur the rejection of their husbands, in favor of younger, not-yet-flawed faces, drove them into expensive and painful erasure of the evidence.

Not Jade. Jade had done nothing. Allowing the first smile lines, forehead creases, age spots. She'd welcomed these small signs, believing that her increasingly mature look would indicate her wisdom and good humor, deeper thoughts. Increased understanding. But, that wasn't how Luc saw it. She didn't know that. She didn't know that what he had loved about her when they'd met, when they'd married

years ago, was her young face. "I saw hope and ex-
pectancy!" he told her now, in his accent. The accent
that had murmured poetry and sensuality in her ear.
The accent that now sounded like the sharp rusty
edge of a table you can't stop scraping against every
time you move through the kitchen. Jade sat with
that for a day on the boat (or a week, she couldn't tell)
and asked him again, then. Not wanting to fight, just
wanting to understand what happened. It couldn't be
her face, gently worn, not too worn yet, from snow
skiing and sailing and just being outside. Just having
adventures, just having fun. It was something else,
right? Something else.

He took her hands. He faced her and took her
hands there in the cabin on the boat with Susie/
Shelly on deck with the rest, the smudges roaming
around. He put his head in her hands, even, and then
sat up again.

"The face is the truth teller." Jade had never before said it this way, but that was really how she felt.
The truth teller. So it was good that people could see
more of her now, the beginnings of the creases and
the sun spots, just the beginnings, but of a good
road, revealing her truth, something good.

"Yes, I agree," Luc began, "the face is the truth
teller, as you say," in his accent, that which was once
sexually electrifying and now a rusty and scraping
kitchen table edge. "But I see a truth in your face,
and I don't want to know it."

18

Jenny. 22. Waitress.

"Ha ha ha, ha ha ha!!!"

Their laughter splashed through the jetway as Jenny and her friends stepped off the plane into the long white tunnel to the gate. Like a basket of freshly cut flowers, still warm from the garden; like a barely unwrapped candy, glassy and colorful; like new cars, with just enough mileage on them to have gotten them to the dealership, these three women walked. Laughing and periodically leaning into one another, their tote bags on a shoulder, in a hand. Strawberry-blond here, chestnut hair there, thick and finger-tamed. Tossed from one side and then the other. Brown leather boots, a pair of heeled sandals, tight jeans, a faux fur vest. And sunglasses, in a hand, stuck atop a head. A requisite, the sunglasses, of course. Laughing, laughing, giddy with expectation of this, finally here, finally, "Yes, we did it." Finally in Los Angeles, California.

Actresses, all of them. Well, almost. Yes, actresses. A commercial here, an on-camera local news report there, a pinch of high school play productions. Yes, actresses. Here now, to really do it, really do what they had been talking about, scheming about, telling everyone they were going to do. "You're so pretty! You should be a movie star," from everyone, just about everyone. They'd found each other. Easily, they'd found each other. "You have to meet Erin," or Kelly, or Jenny, "she's planning on going out to Hollywood someday too!" They met, somehow. Jealous at first; hell yes. The competition, the other prettiest girls in town. But bonded then, with mutual goals, "To Hollywood!"

It would happen, they would make it happen. How could it not happen? They'd been irresistible at home in St. Louis. Everyone there said so. So what, acting classes or college? Maybe a semester done, maybe a year, but no more. What did it matter? They were young and beautiful, everyone said so. Stardom was almost a birthright for the young and beautiful, right? You don't need all that other stuff, the work or education or whatever.

Jenny suddenly pulled out an earbud and held it out to Erin and Kelly on the jetway. "Oh hell yes. THIS SONG. Am I right?" Erin and Kelly paused, halting their forward thrust and energy, there in the narrow passage, blocking the passengers behind them. Paused there and leaned into the earbud to catch the tune of Jenny's song.

"Oh YES!" from Kelly. Erin bobbed her head up and down to the beat and posed her lips in the requisite "duck" shape, signaling musical approval. Jenny then replaced her earbud and the trio continued down the jetway, their excitement mounting. Calls had been made, a small apartment had been rented. Studio City, "Where all the studios are!" The confidence, the manifest destiny of it all. It had made them haughty at home, in St. Louis. Parents had tried to warn them, Erin's parents at least, and Jenny's mother. "Looks fade, sweetie," like salt on snow, threatening to dissolve Jenny's dreams. "You don't know ANYTHING!" she had screamed at her mother, "ANYTHING!" Screamed it at her father too, for being there, for daring to witness such a horrible thing being said to Jenny. Horrible.

As they stepped out of the jetway and into the terminal, Jenny imagined they were all making an entrance, like they do in the movies. Slow motion, hair blown back by an inexplicable wind, some cool music playing. "We have arrived!" It was a movie in her head. They were going to own this town.

Jenny glanced around at the waiting passengers seated at the gate as they passed by. "All hail my youth and beauty!" she thought. It filled her with adrenaline, that thought. But just before the trio exited the gate to traverse past the other gates and restaurants to baggage claim, Jenny noticed another trio coming toward them, to wait at that gate for a departing flight. This new trio was older. Older. 40s or 50s. Polished, but ravaged with anger and disappointment. Unhappy, strained, wrinkled, and tired.

Jenny was startled. She quickly looked behind her at the gate monitor to see where the next plane was headed, this older trio's flight. She hoped like hell it was Rome or Paris or New York. No. Topeka, Kansas. The older trio was going to wait for their flight to Topeka. Only 300 miles from St. Louis.

Jenny looked back at the older trio, and the film in her head, where she and her friends were triumphantly making a wind-blown, slow-motion entrance, changed to something Jenny couldn't stop. The audio of her mother's "Looks fade, sweetie" played in some low, soft, painfully helpful loop inside her, and the visuals were invaded by a sequence from *Moby-Dick*, the only "classic" book she finished in high school. Jenny saw that moment where the *Pequod*, Captain Ahab's whaler, passes by the *Goney*, another whaling ship. The *Goney* is nearing home, after a four-year expedition. The ship has been bleached white by salt and sun and storms, trails of rust stain the hull, her crew long-bearded and haggard from chasing ocean beasts for 1,460 days and nights. The *Pequod*, in contrast, is just starting its expedition, the ship's new paint bold and glistening, her crew full of promise and verve and confidence. Captain Ahab, so energetically possessed with his self-inflicted mission to capture Moby-Dick, is undeterred by the ravaged look of the *Goney* and its crew. He cries out vigorously to the passing *Goney*, "Ship ahoy! Have ye seen the White Whale?"

The blonde in the older trio met Jenny's eyes. It was just for a second, just a second, but it seemed to siphon Jenny's entire stardom life plan. The older blonde appeared to know, looking at Jenny and her friends, appeared to know that Jenny would soon be in her place. Older and discarded, on her way out of LA, passing by another group of young beautiful things, having just arrived. Older Jenny on her way home to St. Louis, having failed to capture what little can be captured in a net of youth and beauty and bravado that has eschewed training and education and the development of skills.

After a moment, Jenny suddenly felt infuriated. Infuriated that this woman, that her mere presence, would dare take away any of her dreams. "I'm nothing like you," she thought. "I am the *Pequod* and not the *Goney*. I will pass you by and ignore your worn-and-torn weariness. I will have nothing to do with you, except to cry out and ask you as we pass, 'Ship ahoy! Have ye seen the White Whale?'"

19

Chris. 32. Actress.

"Chris!"

Chris snapped her head to the right and blinked. After a moment, a large smile broke out on her face.

"Oh my God, you guys. Hiiii!" Too loud in the small audition waiting room. Kiss, kiss, hug, hug. Chris with two of the four women sitting there.

"Sign in, sign in!" Beverly gestured to the audition sign-in sheet in the corner of the room.

"I'm a full twenty minutes late. I'm glad there are people still waiting here. Maybe they won't notice!" Chris laughed a bit as she wrote her information on the sheet.

"Don't worry; they're taking 20 to 30 minutes for each audition. It's taking forever."

"Oh, this is Diana," said Mila. "She's been nice enough to not complain about our totally distracting conversation."

Diana smiled. "It's fine."

Mila pointed to the fourth woman there. "And the one looking over the audition sides is Monica. The only disciplined actress here."

Monica looked up, winked, and moved to a chair by the door to run her lines.

Chris leaned toward Beverly and Mila, and lowered her voice to a hoarse whisper. "So tell me more about the distracting conversation."

"Oh, the usual: how are we going to stop our faces from getting older?"

Chris was surprised. "No . . . C'mon, you both look fantastic."

"We're both 38, girl. Lookin' down the barrel," Beverly joked.

"Actually, 39 here," Mila corrected.

Beverly gave her a look, slightly tinged with alarm. "It's OK . . ." she assured Mila.

"It's a motherfucker, really." A wry smile was on Mila's lips as her hands twisted her audition pages in unconscious emphasis. "I mean, I'm still just as good an actress. Better even, now, and I'm not going out on half the auditions I used to." She pushed her hair back over her ear and straightened up. "I'm trying to stay in gratitude. Stay in gratitude. Hey. I'm glad I'm here. It's been my only audition so far this month."

"But it's cyclical!" Chris offered. "It's busy, then slow, then busy again . . ."

"Yeah, cyclical like life," Beverly chortled. "Birth, then you do some stuff, then you die. End of cycle."

Chris was trying to think of a way to get out of the conversation, and also make the conversation not true at the same time. Either change the conversation so that Beverly and Mila would say that everything gets better and not worse, or make them be quiet about all of this. This hurt her, hurt her that they were saying these things about themselves.

Beverly tapped Mila's forearm. "Chris isn't there yet. She's . . . How old are you?"

"32."

"She's just 32."

"On the edge, though . . ." Mila warned.

"Maybe," Beverly conceded.

Chris bristled at any suggestion that she was aging. She was barely 32; had her birthday last week. "The edge? The edge of what?" she pressed.

"There's this weird chasm . . ." Beverly started.

"Like a river . . ." Mila added.

"Yeah, a river at about 35. It's just not the same after that."

Diana, in her adjacent folding metal chair, looked over at Beverly. "It used to be 30. The river."

"She's right," Mila confirmed.

Diana shrugged her shoulders. "At least it's not until 35 now."

The audition room door opened suddenly and laughter and full-volume chatter poured into the waiting room. The casting directors and the producer ushered the actress out and gave tight smiles to the others waiting there. One of the casting directors consulted the sign-in sheet.

"Monica?" A smile and an inviting arm. Monica

rose and disappeared into the casting room with the group.

"OK, we've got another 40 minutes before any of us are called in," Beverly complained.

"That turning-30 thing . . . it was such a crazy assumption. I got told by a CPA, just before I fired him . . . literally an accountant . . . when I was like 26 . . . He was talking about being protective of my money or whatever and how we want to make sure that I have a lot in savings before I turn 30 and 'hit my expiration date.' I fired him immediately . . . I mean, 26 . . ."

The other women neither confirmed nor denied the accountant's assumption.

"Then there's the whole Russian roulette with the baby timing," offered Mila.

The older women nodded their agreement.

"You guys know Lillian Turner? She did it right. Had her kids at 22 or something. She still hit the river at 35, but at least she wasn't completely out of commission for two years in her early 30s or something with a birth." Diana reapplied her lipstick using a tiny compact mirror. "I had mine at 32, and OK, out of commission for over a year, but you know I had the 'baby lift.' Hell, if I was going to be off the map for that long, at least I could come back with no evidence of the baby or of staying up all night feeding it."

"Really? They did great work." Mila tilted her head to take in Diana's profile.

"Thanks."

"A baby lift, like a tummy tuck?" asked Chris, lightly.

"Oh yeah. Plus. The whole 'Mommy Makeover.' Tummy tuck, breast lift, a little lipo." Diana lifted the front of her shirt to show her stomach. "See, look."

The women regarded her flat stomach. "You can't even see the scar," marveled Beverly. "How soon after the baby can you get that?"

"Six months to a year. I did it after six months. It was fine . . . I did the under-eye bit too. I was starting to get bags."

"Wait, really?" Chris was taken aback.

"Oh yeah." said Diana.

"That's on my list, when I have enough money," pledged Beverly.

"But you're . . . none of you are even 40 yet. I mean, I always thought plastic surgery was something people did in their sixties."

Mila laughed. "Oh honey, no. It's now and always."

Chris felt sick. "But, you're all beautiful. Why would you . . ."

Mila, Beverly, and Diana shared a look. Beverly touched Chris's knee. "Either you build a bridge over the river or you fall into it."

"You're not there just yet, but you'll see. I mean, the work's going to dry up, but at least you can try to mitigate it, buy a few more years." Mila was unfolding her sides. "Jesus, I guess I'd better look at these pages. I think I'm up next."

"Wait. This is just . . . What about Fanny Hoffman, Kira Teller, or Dorothy Bridge? I mean, those are older actresses who work all the time."

"Yeah, there are exactly three 'mature ladies' who work. That's it," said Beverly, with a resigned exhale.

"And they've all had plastic surgery. All of them," added Diane.

"What? Really?"

The door to the casting office opened again and the group thanked Monica as she left.

Mila whispered to Beverly, "Only 15 minutes that time."

The casting director looked at the sign-in sheet. "Mila? You ready?"

"Yes, great." Mila followed the casting director into the other room, as Beverly and Diana both pulled out their audition sides and began to study them.

Chris couldn't, wouldn't, study hers. Chris would later go onto audition for those casting directors and that producer, while consumed with what Beverly and Mila and Diana had said. Distracted by this curse they seemed to place on Chris, this hand-waving assumption that her experience was going to be just like theirs. That Chris was going to "fall off the map," if she had a baby; that Chris was going to work increasingly less; that Chris was going to lie down under someone's anesthesia, someone's scalpel, someone's idea of what she should look like, and have all her visible experience cut away. Chris wished like hell she could go back and not have heard any of that from them, go back to being hopeful about her professional future, her creative options, her vast and open horizons. She wished she could go back in time and not now feel heavy with their pronouncement of her impending crushing. She wished she could go back.

20

Hannah. 51. Dental Assistant.

"ALL NIGHT LONG!"
  "ALL NIGHT LONG!"
  Hannah jumping with the rest. Everyone jumping euphorically in one of those increasingly rare occurrences of unadulterated joy. For no reason except to feel it. Jump, clap, everyone. Why and how did they all start down this waterslide of exuberance here at the wedding? Something in the room; what?

Hannah didn't care. This song, the pure invitation for anyone nearby to jump on a table, take someone's hand, and just dance, remembering nothing of the day, being only in that moment of frivolity. Purposelessly, uninhibited.

Everyone in the room seemed to have inhaled a freedom. And with this song. This song? Why? Even the wedding cover band looked surprised, now blowing their saxophones louder, background singers swinging their hips wider now, the keyboardist banging on his keys harder, to keep this, not let it fly away, keep this excitement, this completely unexpected explosion of happiness and freedom in the room. How did this happen? How could they keep it going, going, going all night?

"ALL NIGHT LONG!"

"ALL NIGHT LONG!"

The bride's father was doing a jig of sorts in an impromptu dance circle, people cheering him on.

"GO, BEN, GO!"

"Daddy!!!!"

"Look at that!"

"KARL, you NEXT!" And on and on.

Hannah jumping and laughing with Jim or Tim . . . Oh, she'd met him so long ago, 25 years ago? A musician, yes. He'd played with some big acts then. A bass player. Played on some lead singer's solo project. Tim, his name was Tim. Hannah's hair was whipping her face with every twist of her head, her throat becoming raw from yelling. Happily, whipped face and raw throat. Happily.

The song ended and a cheer rose up and spread itself through the space. The band quickly segued into another song, another 1980s party anthem. "Let's Hear It for the Boy," or something. Hannah and Tim stayed on the dance floor, smiling, unwilling to sit down and allow the draining of this joy.

"Did you ever see Lionel Richie's music video for that?" Hannah shouted at Tim, over the music. "The town coming together for a dance party. Like, everyone in their sort-of work costumes, the business suit, the construction overalls . . ."

"You always have to have a construction worker! The Village People!"

"Right! And everyone's in pastels or bright colors, headbands and all that. Oh my God, that video is so '80s!!"

Tim closed his eyes in remembrance as they danced. "The '80s! God, I remember meeting you back then! I think I was heavily into my Le Tigre shirt phase."

"Right!"

"Oh, you were so beautiful then!"

Like a shard of metal. Suddenly. Into her face, into her balloon, into her birthday cake. Still smiling, maybe not hearing right, hopefully, maybe heard Tim wrong. "What was that?"

Tim with a broad grin on his face, his spirit still awash with the joy in the room, his eyes half-lidded, swaying to the music. "Yeah!" and leaning to Hannah so she could hear him better, "YOU WERE SO BEAUTIFUL BEFORE!"

The blood drained from Hannah. She felt it move from her face and torso down to her legs. Maybe her body did that so that even with her brain stuttering its function now, at least her legs would still have the energy they needed to keep her upright.

Hannah looked at him, with a furrow in her brow now, questioning. But Tim, Tim still with that beatific smile on his face, still swaying to the music, still consumed with that joy in the room. Unaffected, unapologetic, unrepentant, serene.

Hannah stared at him. Nothing from him. No "Oh shit, I'm sorry. That must have sounded horrible." Or "Oh! I meant that you're *still* beautiful." Something. No, nothing. Hannah, still dancing, still a smear of a smile on her face, still. Looking at Tim, at his absolute lack of remorse. Tim, older than her by five years or so. Not much of a looker, just some ordinary, plain guy.

Hannah felt horrified. Was it so matter-of-fact, so obvious that she was older, no longer beautiful now, ugly even? So matter-of-fact that she was once beautiful and now so hideous that people have no compunction about saying it as a fact? Like, "Your hair used to be blond" or "You used to live down the street from me" and now she didn't? So matter-of-fact like that?

"Let's hear it for the boy!" sang the wedding band.

"LET'S GIVE THE BOY A HAND!" from the dance floor.

"Let's hear it for my baby!" the singer answered.

Maybe Hannah was looking at this all wrong. Tim seemed to be completely unaware that he'd said anything offensive. Maybe he was just making a statement of fact and whether someone looks older now or less beautiful or taller or fatter or paler meant nothing to him. Maybe these things were not any measure of worth to him. They were of no real importance perhaps, just observations, like those

a child might make. She watched Tim, in his bliss-
ful state, his moving of his legs and his arms and
his head to the music. Hannah was so used to this
societal measure of worth wherein calling a woman
young-looking and beautiful was the highest compliment she could be paid. And calling a woman old
or ugly or tired was the most vile insult. Maybe none
of that was accurate, at all. Maybe Tim, in his odd
little bass-player life, was an anomaly, exposing the
incorrectly high pedestal on which we'd all placed
youthful looks and beautiful faces. Maybe Tim was
the only one who was really seeing those things for
what they are.

21

Esther. 67. Former Sales Manager.

Pencil skirt. Esther didn't know why she put that on today. Once in a while, she just felt compelled to wear it. Pencil skirt in a light green, stockings (not very modern, but a sensual throwback for her now), her ivory pumps, a white blouse. Nice. Such a clean and fresh look, at any age. She was in the mood today. It didn't hurt that no other skirt in her closet made her derrière look quite so good.

Esther exhaled through pursed lips, as she flipped through her mail, on the small table by the front door. She could pay her dry cleaning bill in person today; that would be a good outing. And order new checks at the counter at the bank. "It's good to get out in the world. Keeps me young," was her patented line to others. Esther felt that too many people used the mail or online conveniences for nearby tasks that could be done in person. "They're missing out on the human experience!" she would tell her friends when the subject of the younger generation came up, and it came up often.

She put her blond hair in a smart bun and then changed her mind and let it fall onto her shoulders.

Her side part had always been her signature, and it was most fetching when the hair was down, such that it created a curtain over her right eye. "Veronica," they used to call her at school, "Veronica Lake." Esther picked her gold, shell-shaped clip-on earrings and snapped them gently onto her ears. Such a fine figure she cut. Still. As her friends became "old women," one by one, Esther still retained her figure, her style, her grace. Good genes, she supposed. She'd mention this as a defense when people would compliment her. She'd shrug and say, "Just good genes, I guess!" She worked at it too. Sure. She ate well, swam at the nearby pool three times a week, and solved the crossword puzzle every day (well, most days) to keep her mind sharp. She helped it along, so it couldn't have been just good genes. Esther knew that, but liked to say it anyway; her way of bragging gently.

What a beautiful day! Esther stepped out of her apartment building, waving goodbye to the doorman there in the lobby, at his narrow marble desk. Spring had sprung. She thanked God that she'd never had an issue with pollen allergies, as she inhaled the lilac and jasmine, and marveled at the blossoms in the trees. Pink and white and purple. Beautiful! She knew if she walked down Second Avenue, she'd see those cherry trees in full bloom. It was a bit out of her way, but it was worth the trouble. Puppies happily straining against their leashes, children running, laughing in the playground at the corner school, couples drinking coffee on restaurant patios; the sidewalk was a trek through a wonderful amusement park ride of joy.

Esther lengthened her stride, wanting to feel the blood pump through her legs, to add to the exhilaration of the day. She made a left and then a right down Second Avenue. Two more blocks and there they were. Oh, what a sight! Four cherry blossom trees, at the height of their soft and impossible beauty. A new addition last year, in the courtyard of a recently finished, modern business building. The breeze swept almost imperceptibly through the trees and caused a delicate sprinkling of petals, a first snow of sorts; the kind that melts before it hits the ground, but serves as a promise of a forthcoming and dense powdered-sugar descent in coming days.

She turned from the blossoms and continued down the sidewalk, back over to Third Avenue, toward the dry cleaners. She was almost past the construction site when she heard the cat calls, from the construction workers two stories above.

"FOXY MAMA!" they yelled. "WOWZA." A couple of whistles. Flattering, so flattering, a perfect addition to her walk of joy. Getting out in the world and interacting. Esther was right, see? It does a soul good to get out.

"How about a drink?!" from one worker. Esther

giggled to herself. What if she said yes? They certainly wouldn't expect that.

Esther stopped there on the sidewalk, smiled, and turned to face them. "Well, what time?" she was going to say. That was the plan. Take them up on it and see what they did. They'd probably squirm and elbow each other, and just maybe, one of them would yell, "I get off at 6!"

But, no.

Esther stopped there on the sidewalk, and smiled, and turned, and parted her lips to speak. As she tossed her curtain of hair off her right eye, she heard, "EWWW, GROSS!"

Ew. About her. About her face. The one thing they had not seen clearly when she strutted by, energetically, invigorated, and happy.

Ew, gross. She stood there for a moment, adjusting to the vast difference between her plan and the reality there. The construction workers stared back. Three of them boldly, and two of them now looking away, out of embarrassment or disinterest, Esther didn't know which.

Gross. Esther finally inhaled and turned back around, shame blooming over her cheeks. Shame and embarrassment.

She walked. Walked to the dry cleaners to pay her bill. Walked to the bank to order new checks. And walked home. She greeted the doorman and stepped into the elevator. She pressed the button to her floor and watched the polished brass doors come together. She looked at her reflection there, in the brass, and started to laugh.

"Jesus! I guess I'm old now!"

22

Joanne. 54. Textile Designer.

He didn't call her back. Said he would. Thought he would. But, didn't.

Joanne wasn't surprised, just disappointed. They had connected, liked the same food, the same films, had the same criticisms of society. The same. But, no call.

She looked at the rows and rows of books, in the stacks, in the library. The big one, the main library, where the rare volumes sat, in their faded leather covers. She pulled a random book off the shelf, opened it, and inhaled the fragrant decay of paper and ink. Joanne loved that smell.

He was 32. Yes, she knew that it was unlikely, but he had pursued her. She, knowing it was unlikely, knowing he would maybe pull back or question himself or become repulsed that she was older. But no. Joanne didn't really think that any of these guys, these 30-year-old guys, were repulsed by her. They hit on her, didn't they? Over and over, like some conspiracy, men in their 30s were continuously approaching her. To buy her a drink, get some dinner, go on a date. She went, almost always said yes. Had a few long relationships, but then they'd go. First say they never wanted kids, the age difference didn't matter. But then it did. She understood. Maybe that was the reason, them now wanting kids, but maybe not.

She replaced the book on the wood shelf and continued down the aisle. Collections, collections of information, of verbal cadence, of customs you can't find online. Captured like pressed flowers between the worn fabric covers. Old magazines and trade papers bound in tall, faded-green book bindings, where the articles sat alongside the ads of the time. In context, in context.

Maybe it *was* her face, creased and drooping slightly. Loose skin draping the sinewy neck muscles, crepey skin resting on the elbow, just inside, where the forearm meets the bicep, where the skin used to be smooth and taut. There. All of it. Maybe that was the truth.

Joanne's father once told her that men's desire for youthful-looking women was all about procreation. That it was a part of evolution we can't get around. That they'd *all* want her as a baby oven, so sit back and look at the options. A real seller's market, he used to say. "They'll all want to buy what you're selling, so take your time and pick who *you* want, and let the others slide." She did, she had, picked the best guy there, in her 20s. And then found, ironically, she couldn't have children. Ironically.

Mike died anyway. It was a happy marriage, with her ironically unable to conceive and him dying so young: it had been a happy marriage. Then, growing into herself, in her early 40s. Moving to Chicago, taking that dream job, unencumbered by a husband or children. Loving the job. Freeing, fantastic, fun life in Chicago. Trips to New York and Los Angeles for work. Often. Maybe it was the freedom she lived with, the lack of responsibilities to an immediate family that shone like a porch light for the 30-year-old men, coming to her like summer moths.

She found her book on a metal shelf, in the research section: a personal record of the American Indians of the Northwest in the 1840s, the only copy she'd been able to track down. She pulled the dense burgundy book from the shelf and started back to the heavy maple-wood table where the rest of her books sat.

If her face and her body were of value to others, to males, just as a means by which the population could continue, was her now creased face and crepey skin a message to males that the baby oven was no longer in operation? "Don't waste your time, you're not going to continue the species with this one. She's done; her sole purpose has expired."

Joanne smiled to herself. She liked how the smooth-faced, taut-skinned young face and body of her 20s tricked all those young men into thinking she could help them spread their seed, fulfill their evolutionary duty, guarantee the continuation of their particular collection of DNA. Yeah, not Joanne. And the irony, another irony, was that young men (though not as young) were still banging themselves up against her, older now, porch light.

"Attractive." At the enormous 3,000-page dictionary there in the library, by the bank of computers, Joanna thumbed through to find the word "attractive": *1. Pleasing or appealing to the senses. 2. Appealing to look at; sexually alluring. 3. Having beneficial qualities or features that induce someone to accept what is being offered.* That last one, #3, was the best one to her.

She felt sad for the men now, for what seemed to be a muffled understanding of their attraction to her. Her father's theory, inhaled by society, had trained these men on the first two definitions of "attraction": *pleasing to the senses; appealing to look at; sexually alluring*. When all the while, they had (also? actually?) been led by the third definition; they had been induced by her *beneficial qualities*. Unconsciously, maybe unconsciously.

She sat down at the table, with the rest of her research books. Maybe flying in the face of the first two definitions and choosing the third would cause a man to be misunderstood by other men. Maybe just following an attraction to a woman who adheres to the third definition instead, wherein there's an attraction that presses deeper, past childbearing possibilities or the appearance thereof, could cause a man to be cast out by other men. Well then, maybe the choice of a mate is not about the woman at all, but rather about that man's desire to maintain inclusion with the other men.

Joanne leaned back in her chair and and looked over the rest of the people there in the library, hunched over their own piles of research. In the far corner sat a man, about 35 or so, wearing a hoodie, his pen paused midsentence above his notebook. He was looking at Joanne, longer than one should. She looked back at him, longer than one should, and smiled.

23

Beth. 58. Model.

"She's stunning."

"And hasn't had any work done."

Theresa, the younger of the three, was surprised. "That's natural?"

"I know. Some people are just lucky like that." Meredith teed up her ball, straightened her back, and gestured to Beth as she approached. "Every wrinkle is her own. Even the bags under her eyes."

Beth neared, swinging a golf club loosely by her side. "Sorry I'm late!"

"No problem!" Meredith took a big swipe and they all watched her ball arc up and then fall to the grass. Meredith turned back to them and winked.

Sheila applauded lightly, impressed, and then turned to Beth. "We were just telling Theresa here what a natural beauty you are. That your wrinkles and eye bags are all *you*."

Beth smiled at Theresa, accentuating her crow's feet and smile lines. "Oh, you'll get there. You just have to be patient, give your beauty time to blossom. You're not using sunscreen or anything, are you?"

Theresa made a shameful face. "A little bit, just for the anti-cancer benefits."

Beth nodded. "That's understandable . . . Well, like I said, just give your face time to crease and relax. Before you know it, your face will blossom into something fantastic."

Sheila considered Theresa. "She looks like a young Georgia O'Keeffe, doesn't she?"

Theresa put her hand on her chest. "Oh my God. I hope I'm that lucky to wind up looking like her. Wow, thank you. Really."

"I just call it like I see it."

"You know, Sheila discovered me." Beth threw a golf ball up and caught it.

"Are you going to tee off or juggle?" said Sheila, laughing.

"Oh, I'll tee off. Don't you worry." Beth leaned down to place the ball. "Sheila spotted me in a fabric store, if you can believe it." She stood up and squinted down the fairway.

"Ha! I was there, remember? I watched it happen," added Meredith.

"Oh yeah. When Sheila first walked up to us, I thought for sure she was going to offer *you* some kind of contract." Beth swung and whacked the ball far from them.

Meredith waved her hand at Beth. "Oh, c'mon. I'm not half as beautiful as you. My eyelids don't even droop yet."

Sheila placed her ball. "Now Meredith is a beauty, that's true, but she's not quite ripe yet." She pulled her club back and released it, smashing her ball into the air. "But Meredith, in a few years, you come see me, all right? Your face is certainly headed in the right direction."

Theresa hurriedly placed her ball. "So, Sheila saw you in the fabric store, and then what?"

"Oh, right! I was there getting some fabric for my daughter's senior prom dress—she wanted something 'handmade'—and Sheila walked right up to me and said—"

"You're gorgeous and you know it. Come work for me and I can make you millions," Sheila cut in.

"No!" from Theresa.

"That's exactly what she said!" from Meredith.

"Wow. And how soon after that did you have your first magazine cover?"

"Tee off, girl!"

"OK, OK." Theresa swung at the ball and the four of them watched it fly for a moment.

"Great. Let's go." The women turned from the sight.

"So, was your first cover right after that?"

They climbed into the golf cart as Beth considered the question. "I . . . I think it was that Gucci campaign first, wasn't it, Sheila?"

"Gucci and also Chanel, for fragrance only."

Meredith guided the cart down the path. "She was 52."

"I got her right as she was blooming!" Sheila tightened her leather gloves. "One more year and she would have had all the big modeling agencies after her. I got lucky."

Theresa leaned in from the backseat. "What advice would you give me? I'm only 30, but I want to look my best later."

"I know the plastic surgery route is tempting, but don't do it," warned Meredith.

"It always looks fake," confirmed Beth, from beside her.

Sheila turned around in her seat to look at Theresa. "Look, some of the models I've got have probably done a little work, to make themselves look older. Some repetitive facial motion here, some weathered resurfacing there, but the best way to go is au naturel. Spend time at the beach or on a sailboat; get a sunburn. Skiing is great too." Meredith and Beth nodded their heads in agreement. "And don't shy away from facial expressions at both ends of the spectrum. The laughing *and* the crying . . ."

"Oh, crying is the best," said Beth suddenly. "I cried really hard just before the shoot for my last *Vogue* cover and the editor said it was the most breathtaking cover she'd ever published."

"Oh, the April issue?! Where you're on that black sand beach?"

"Yes, exactly."

"Everyone looks great right after they've cried hard," added Meredith.

The cart stopped at Beth's ball, near the sandpit. The women stepped out and Sheila squeezed Beth's shoulder. "But no one quite gets that puffy under-eye look after crying like Beth does."

Beth squared herself up with her ball. "Oh, c'mon. I can't take all this praise." She swung her club and looked out, disappointed at its arc. "I swear to God, you guys are just trying to distract me from the game."

"Well, it's the truth, you are stunning!" yelled Meredith from across the way, as she let her swing crack into the ball. "Though I'd love to win back that money you won on the last game."

"You've got your chance!" Beth yelled back. "Just play better!"

Meredith laughed and flipped her off as they made their way back to the cart, where Sheila and Theresa sat. "I'm gunning for you, Beth Weinberg. My neck skin is really loosening up lately. I'm going to call Sheila someday, and then we'll see who's booking all the magazine covers."

"OK! Can't wait!" Beth and Meredith climbed into the golf cart and Sheila sped away, down the path, to the balls, once more.

24

Jessica. 27. Retail Store Cashier.

"If she's smoking hot and rich, OK. Yeah, that can work."

"Forties? Fifties?"

"Yeah, sure! Some old hag who's going to pay for everything? Sure." Laughter, laughter.

Jessica looked at her boyfriend to see if he was agreeing with Marcus. Chad had an eager look on his face. She knew he would. Expectant and eager. Especially for whatever Marcus had to say. She rolled her eyes to herself.

Brianna was pressing Marcus again. "So 40s or 50s, no problem if they pay. And the poor ones?"

"Can suck my . . ." Marcus started.

"Jesus, Marcus."

Chad was stifling a laugh. Stifling for Jessica's sake. Otherwise, he'd make that laugh as loud as possible.

"What can I get you guys?" The waitress was there, older, attractive. Jessica thought she remembered her from when she'd worked there as the hostess. Becky? Carrie?

Marcus grabbed a menu to look at it again. "Hold on . . ."

"The turkey burger," from Jessica.

"I'll have the ribs."

"Can I get the Caesar salad with no croutons?"

"Oh, get them on the side, I'll eat them." Jessica handed back her menu as Brianna added, "On the side," to the waitress. *Becky* was on her name tag.

Becky looked at Marcus, there studying the menu. "And you? What are you having?"

"Don't you have that bacon cheeseburger anymore?"

"It's there. Is that what you'd like?"

"Where?" Marcus, still searching the menu.

Becky stuck her order pad and pencil back in her apron pocket. "It's just under sandwiches now. I have it down on your order." She reached out for the menu.

Marcus kept scanning for another couple of seconds until he found it. "Oh! Yeah, over here." He then handed back the menu, slightly flustered. "Pretty stupid to move it. What's the point?"

Becky smiled a tight smile and walked away with the menus.

"Bitch," Marcus muttered under his breath.

"She was just taking your order. What'd she do wrong?" Brianna's voice sounded tired of this habitual restaurant behavior from Marcus.

"It's not like she needed the menu," offered Chad in Marcus's defense.

Marcus took a sip of his Coke and leaned forward over the table. "This is what I'm talking about. These old cows have this attitude, this tone just like all those older women when I was growing up. And then you want to know if I think they're attractive? Am I supposed to be attracted to someone who's just like the women I hated? That old bitch teacher, Monroe, who gave me an F and fucked up my year? Made me retake that class over the summer? Damn."

Jessica was quiet. Brianna had her arms crossed and was committed to looking out the window. Chad, of course, was offering Marcus a sympathetic and thoughtful look, encouraging him to continue.

"They ruined my life. Sabotaged me. Every chance they got, they smothered my success. Just tossed me into poverty and struggle, over and over." Marcus flicked a sugar packet across the table at no one. It landed on the booth seat between Chad and Jessica. "That bitch teacher, Monroe; that nightshift manager, Connie. There's lots of them. They make me want to throw up. Taking advantage of people younger than them and telling them what to do . . . I'm supposed to give these women a break now and be attracted to them?" He took another sip of his Coke. "Name one man who wants to date bosses and teachers and principals who ruined their lives for multiple years."

Jessica blinked. "But, those were other people." Chad shot her a look. "I mean, that doesn't make all older women unattractive . . ."

Marcus sat back in the booth, pulled one knee up, and let an arm dangle on top of it. Head tilted back, he regarded her through half-lidded eyes. He smiled slightly. "So you think I should just be attracted to these types that caused the problems in the first place? Hmm. You're wrong. You don't know what you're talking about. As long as money defines a man, right? Or success. That was set up a long time ago. Wake up. So, if the man doesn't come up with money or success, he broke some social contract, see?"

Becky arrived with their food, a plate in each hand and two more stacked on her forearms. Onto the table, in front of each of them. Marcus grabbed the ketchup as Brianna pushed the small dish of croutons toward Jessica.

Marcus eyed Becky sideways as she left the table, then he looked at Jessica. "80 percent of men are unsuccessful. Grew up that way, blocked by these 'helpful' bitches. So if you want men to be interested in older women after that, be attracted to them and all that, you better consider what's being offered to us."

25

Gwenyth. 39. Mother.

Yes. She had done it all. Really dug in, immersed herself. Found her calling, you could say. Hadn't felt like her life had much of a purpose. Then, found it. Immediately, with the birth of her twins. Kira and Frederick. Fraternal. Beautiful. Breast-feeding, with a night nurse. Yes, lucky enough to afford one of those. Necessary. How could she have done that without help? Two babies. Her husband, Garth, was a help, but he had his job, and traveling for it to boot. But Gwenyth was in her right place, she felt it. Took the twins everywhere. Everyone said she made it look so easy. It was, Gwenyth supposed, because she'd really found her purpose. She knew this wasn't true for a lot of women, to feel this way about motherhood, and that was fine. She was fine with that.

Gwenyth had played the twins classical music in the womb and felt that because of that, they could really appreciate the string quartet concerts she took them to at the park every Saturday. Yes, there were also the Mommy and Me classes, the art classes, the swim classes, of course. But also the trips to the museum, the tours of the fish market, and the book readings. Every Wednesday at the library, in the green felt-paneled reading room. In the winters, they even had the old fireplace lit. The twins heard every fairy tale, every fable. Most often it was from the older text and not the modern Disneyfied version. The real culture. She wanted the twins to have real culture. Someday Gwenyth would take them to Germany or France, so they could see all those storybook towns. That would be delightful.

This past Wednesday, though, Gwenyth had an upsetting experience. The twins, now old enough to be reading on their own almost, were still enjoying someone reading to them. A comfort, Gwenyth was sure. She had arrived, just like she had for years, all the other Wednesdays, with her double stroller and her beautiful twins. They'd taken their seats on the floor with the other children and mothers, and waited for the reading. After a few minutes, out came a woman, a new woman. Not Annie, the child development grad student who had led these readings since Gwenyth and the twins started coming. No, a new woman. An old woman. White hair, up in a bun, some strands attractively loose around her face and at her neck. She wore a smart black sweater and gray slacks. She was reading the Brothers Grimm's "Jorinda and Joringel," one of Gwenyth's favorites. "There was once an old castle in the midst of a large and thick forest, and in it a witch dwelt all alone. In the day-time she changed herself into a cat or a screech-owl, but in the evening she took her proper shape again as a human being. She could lure wild beasts and birds to her, and then she killed and boiled and roasted them. The men who neared the witch's castle would be paralyzed, and the women would be turned into birds the witch kept in cages."

As the older woman read aloud, Gwenyth kept the twins busy with Cheerios she had in a small bag. After a few moments, Kira's lip started trembling. Frederick followed suit and started crying, with fear in his eyes. Gwenyth tried to calm them, but she didn't know what had gone wrong. The twins always loved story time here. Kira let out a wail and the other mothers nearby carefully pulled their children to themselves.

"Kira, what is it, baby? What happened? Does something hurt?" Gwenyth urgently cooed.

Frederick pointed at the old woman reading the story and declared, at a volume that would cause Gwenyth to never again return to this wonderful story time, "THE WITCH!"

Kira wailed again and turned away from the old woman.

A few of the other kids now saw the old woman through the twins' eyes, and started their own lip trembles and wailing.

Mortified, Gwenyth started gathering her things to leave. As she reached her hands out to the twins, to guide them out of the room, to the stroller, she was immediately struck by something she could not undo. The witch from *Snow White*, the witch from *Sleeping Beauty,* the wicked stepmother from *Cinderella*, the old woman from *Hansel and Gretel*, the witch from *The Little Mermaid*. All of them, the villains in these stories, were old women. Gwenyth's face flushed as she led the twins out by the hands, her activity bag slung over her shoulder, the reading room now in emotional disarray. The children frightened, the mothers embarrassed and frustrated, the older woman reader mortified.

Gwenyth knew she had made an error that would not be unwound. She had drilled it into her children, week after week, almost their entire lives, that to be an older woman is to be evil, is to be reviled. Her son, only now starting to feel his masculinity, bonding with his father over smashing rocks and the rest. Her innocent, precious son would one day look at his older female teachers, his bosses, his coworkers, and be repulsed. Out of protection, out of a sense of protecting himself from harm from these bad people, these crones. And her daughter, her beautiful, funny, creative daughter, would someday hate herself because she had turned into one of them, resembling a witch, just by virtue of aging. And perhaps she would someday have a child point at her and scream, "THE WITCH!"

26

Talia. 46. Musical Act Booker.

He'd looked at her a few times. Turned back and looked down the way at her. Smiled slightly, or seemed like he was contemplating a smile, in that sultry way, where the eyes start it, but the face doesn't allow the mood to erupt on the lips. Talia's friend Janie was noticing. Gave her the big eyebrow raise and the smirk. Even toasted her, clinking plastic stadium beer cups together with her.

"PEANUTS! KETTLE CORN!" The stadium vendor climbed the stairs once again, past Talia's seat.

The guy, he was late 20s, early 30s, suddenly leaned from the middle of the section, toward the vendor, toward Talia, from the row in front of Talia. "How much?" he yelled to the vendor.

"Either one, 10 dollars."

"Peanuts." The guy reached over, behind his seat and over, and passed a 20 along to Janie, who in turned passed it to Talia, who swapped it for a bag of peanuts and 10-dollar bill. She felt the guy staring at her; the guy pleased that he was making her get the peanut bag for him. She smiled slyly as she passed the bag to Janie and watched it make its way down the seats and jump a row in front, to the guy.

"AND, IT'S OUT OF HERE!" bellowed the stadium announcer. Talia and Janie and the guy and his friends and the rest of the stadium rose to their feet to excitedly watch the baseball arc high and clear and descend on the other side of the wall, where the parking lot started. The guy and his friends all high-fived, and the guy caught Talia's eye as she high-fived Janie.

Talia saw him. And she also saw the confused, maybe just bemused at this point, scowl growing on the guy's friend's face. The friend wore a blue satin team jacket and held a half-filled beer in his fist. When he and the guy sat down finally, Blue Jacket elbowed him.

"Are you looking at *her?*"

The guy smiled slightly, shrugged slightly, "Yeah . . ."

Blue Jacket squinted his eyes and looked closely at the guy, as if squinting would help him hear the guy better. "Why?"

The guy shrugged again and made a face to get Blue Jacket off the topic. Blue Jacket pinched the front of the guy's T-shirt. He'd meant to grab it, take a handful of fabric, but the situation wasn't serious enough for that. "Dude, she's like your mother or your grandmother."

This bit, because Talia had seen the deliberate way Blue Jacket was confronting the guy, this bit Talia heard. Even a row back and five seats over, she heard it. Not all of it, but by some magnetic auditory ability, she picked up "mother" and "grandmother." Yes. She heard that bit.

Something ugly, something sneered, just a little. Like a bit of maple syrup that slides down the side of the bottle after, no matter how carefully you've poured. Something to be licked off, in a guilty-pleasure indulgence. Or, if left on the bottle, on the shelf, something sticky and problematic; a siren song to the ants in the walls, awaiting such a call.

Talia didn't look over at the guy, not right away. She tried to shake the words off her skin first. She didn't look anything like a grandmother. Long black hair, big gold hoop earrings, jeans, and a team hoodie with her favorite player's name and number on the back. Single, divorced, never had kids. A life on the road as a rock band manager, and now a musical act booker for one of the larger arenas in town. Not a mother, not a grandmother. Not.

The guy wouldn't look back at Talia. He had flicked Blue Jacket's fingers off his shirt, and put his attention back on the game. But Blue Jacket leaned toward him and pressed his voice just above the crowd: "That's like incest, man. INCEST."

Blood rose in the guy's cheeks. Talia could see that. She looked at the game now too, put her attention there as well. Forgetting the flirting just a little while ago. Forgetting.

"IF THEY DON'T WIN, IT'S A SHAME!"

When she looked over again, during the seventh-inning stretch, the guy was focused squarely on the field and on half-singing the song and half-drinking the beer that Blue Jacket had just handed him.

"IT'S ONE, TWO, THREE STRIKES YOU'RE OUT . . ."

She could see that syrup bottle going back on the shelf in his mind, the dribble of "She's like your MOTHER" and "She's like your GRANDMOTHER" and "It's like INCEST" glistening on the slick of the glass bottle, now going into the dark cupboard to sit there and wait.

"AT THE OLD BALL GAME!"

The ants would come, from inside the guy's walls. The ants of conformity and fear would come and cover that bottle. And the guy, not knowing what to do, not knowing that a bit of water could wash all that off, would soon take the bottle and lower it, covered with ants, into the trash.

27

Veronica. 43. Professor.

"How did we get here?" Veronica half-watched today's film. A black-and-white Italian drama from the '60s she'd seen many times before. "How did we get to this spot?"

She eyed the backs of her students' heads from the rear of the auditorium. About half were actually watching the movie. The other half were sleeping or poking around on their phones, their screens dimmed. Every quarter, on the first day of class, Veronica would read the syllabus out loud. Almost none of the students ever read it beforehand, in spite of them having had it for a month already. She knew this. So, she would read it out loud, all the professors did. Ran through and emphasized all the rules and requirements, "no cell phone use during screenings" and all that, "as it's disruptive to the course and to the other students," blah, blah. She knew some weren't listening when she read it, or weren't there at all on the first day, or didn't care about the rules. She'd stopped worrying about it. They were going to get the grades they deserved. Every quarter. "Put in the work you want rewarded," she'd say. It was their choice.

On the screen, an older actress gazed at the other actor, shadows from the clouds above passing over her face. She tilted her head up to allow the shadows to fully brush her face.

"How did we get so far away from these kind of films?" Veronica supposed most of her students were not the target audience for this film, with its older actresses and a lack of explosions, guns, and vapid female characters. Some of the guys in this class were serious about filmmaking, but she knew many of them were just there to get a required culture GE out of the way, and that "watching movies all day" sounded easy to them.

Veronica didn't blame modern filmmakers for catering to this young male demographic: the superhero movies, car chase film sequels, violent revenge films . . . She knew the research, had conducted some of it herself, even. Young males between the ages of 15 and 30 years old outnumbered the other filmgoer types two to one on a film's opening weekend. With an opening weekend constituting a third of a film's total box office much of the time, who wouldn't make movies for these guys? Filmmaking is a business.

But the thing that bothered Veronica the most was that because of this catering to this demographic in American film, many of the female parts were simply a reflection of what that young, male group wanted in a woman. They weren't older women, and they often weren't a true reflection of how real women thought or felt at all.

She sat in the last row and put her feet up on the seat in front of her, where no one could see. Yes, these character parts. "The Ideal Woman" of a time, of an era. In the 1920s, it was the Party Girl, the Flapper. In the '30s, it was the Good Woman, the one who was going to make everything OK, for the men, for the families, as the Depression crushed the jobs necessary for the man to feel he was properly fulfilling his proscribed role. In the '40s, it was the Pinch Hitter, the Sacrificer. The men were away at war, and the women back home, filling in the jobs, going to the movies; they watched the female characters toiling away, making strides. An anomaly in the eras, actually: films still created by men, but largely catered to women.

One of the students was coming up the aisle, carrying her backpack and jacket, hunched over so as to not obstruct other students' view of the film, She whispered hoarsely to Veronica as she passed, "Remember I said I had to leave early? I e-mailed you . . ." Veronica smiled her assent and the girl continued out the door, briefly splashing light into the dark auditorium.

In the '50s, when the men returned from war, the pendulum of male-focused movies swung back to its more accustomed spot, and the female character role was the Housewife; moved off of the jobs performed while the men were at war, now the ideal woman was tending to the returned man's needs. In the next decade, men (and women) were experimenting with drugs and sex, and the female character in the films of the '60s needed to be the Free-Love Devotee, the Available Sexual Partner. The '70s appeared to confuse men about everything and it seemed as if the female film characters had to answer for that: the Whore, the Prostitute, the One Who Has to Pay the Price. The 1980s brought a focus on money and greed, so the appropriate companion for the men in film at the time was the Ice Queen, the Rich Bitch, Something to Win or Attain. Men in the '90s seemed to step into (or out of) some kind of self-awareness fog, wanting to be nurturing, not wanting to be macho, and so entered the Strong Female Equal. Men's political confusion of the 2000s birthed the Woman Who's Not Really There at All, and also the Manic Pixie Woman and the Quirky Nonsexual Oddball.

The Italian black-and-white film on the screen ended and Veronica reached up behind her on the wall and flipped the light switches. The students started filing out, backpacks and jackets, out the two doors by the screen, out the doors in the back of the auditorium.

Veronica stood up to get her things near the front desk. The 2010s—what were men now, generally? What kind of woman did they need to see on-screen now. The Girlfriend? Well, that was evergreen. The

Occasional, Accompanying Female Superhero? Veronica thought it would be hard to tell just yet. It would be easier in a few years, in retrospect, to see just what filmmakers catering to young males thought they needed. She was sure they'd settle on some type of nurturer, or some kind of whore. Veronica didn't care, really. She had her viewing niche, her fabulous metaphoric European films of the '50s and '60s, where the women filled the screen with creases and dark circles and pathos on their faces. Maybe Veronica was ignorant, and she was just unknowingly watching the European filmmakers' ideas of the type of women European men wanted, and not some pure representation of women at all. Maybe. But Veronica felt more at home in those films, with the unique-looking and passionate women, than she ever felt with most of the American female film characters, squarely facing and filling some need for the male character. No, Veronica couldn't relate to that at all.

28

Silvie. 31. Graphic Designer.

Dear Ms. Darvich,

I was a big fan years ago and you had a real impact on me. My teens were virtually soaked in your action adventure films ("Agent Frost" forever!) and your personal style. I'm sure you hear this all the time, but my friends and I all bleached our hair once to look like yours, and we also tried to imitate all your outfits. We never did get your effortlessly-messy-hair look down, and our clothes were always the awkward version of your terrific outfits. (One time, I went to a school dance wearing one of my dad's work blazers, tights, and heels, just like when you wore your boyfriend's big tuxedo jacket, stockings, and satin pumps to the Oscars in 1997. My mom made me wear a T-shirt and gym shorts underneath mine, though, and that ruined the whole effect.)

I'm 31 now and I have to admit that I haven't been keeping up with your acting career lately. (I should have been! Shame on me. :) Anyway, I think you're great and I just wanted to send a note about something. I know people have been really critical of your face lately (I mean, we're ALL getting older) and I was thinking about that. I looked you up online, because I wanted to disagree with the press or the bloggers or the general public (whoever had done this) about your older face. I've always felt that anyone can criticize anything, even a cute puppy or a beautiful sunset, but that doesn't make the criticism true. So, I looked up the images of you that they were criticizing, and of course the photos were poorly lit and had caught you at unflattering angles. It was ridiculous, really, and not fair at all.

Then, I saw that new ad campaign you did for that Japanese luggage company and I hated that they smoothed your face out like that. I don't know if it was because it's a luggage company, and that's the luggage business culture's aesthetic, but I hated that they just erased all the character in your face. What I really hope, and please don't be offended, is that that wasn't something you had asked for. I'd hate to think that you asked them to do that to the photo because all those criticisms have turned you into someone who wants people to think you have a smooth face. I mean, I think it must have been that luggage company, because you've never had plastic surgery or fillers, and I love that about you.

There was something else I saw, though, when I looked at other pictures of you online, and it's the reason I'm writing. I don't know if it was the photos they had picked or something going on inside you (crossing my fingers that it's the former), but you look

like these criticisms about your face have really af-
fected you. I'm not famous and I have no idea what
it's like to be watched by everyone all the time, but I
hate thinking that maybe the criticisms have ground
you down or crushed your spirit. The more images of
you I saw, the more I got this feeling, and I'm really
wanting it to not be true. I did find one recent image
where you're with your daughter at the park and you
had that confident attitude again, your expression,
your hair wild, your outfit beyond stylish. It gave me
hope that all those bad comments have not actually
crushed your spirit.

Again, forgive me for speaking so frankly to you
about this, and I sincerely hope I am not offending
you, but this is really affecting me. When I was a
teen, and watching your movies and seeing you in
the press, your confidence changed me. I could see
that you weren't the most beautiful actress, but your
confidence and your attitude were so much bigger
than anyone else's that it made you the most attrac-
tive person ever. And the reason it affected me and
my friends so much was that we weren't the prettiest
girls in school either, but we knew we could have that
very attractive confidence because you had it. And
it worked. I don't know how, but we really became
pretty, if you want to call it that. It was like the confi-
dence just neutralized people thinking we were any-
thing but the cutest girls at school. So, thank you for
that. I don't know if you ever knew that was happening.

But, now there's something maybe going on that wants to topple that confidence I got from you. When I was younger, I could look to you as kind of a beacon or a lighthouse for how to handle what was coming up, because you were 20 years older than me. Your casual cowboy wedding in the mountains, the way you never conformed to that "mommy look" after you had your daughter. You've just continued to be that same confident and stylish individual over the years. (I'm getting married next year and may have kids a year or two after that, so I'm glad to know that I don't have to do the standard wedding or wear mommy clothes like most people do, because I've had you to watch.)

The way you look now, though, is scaring me. And it's not your physical face, not your older look that all these people have been criticizing (so sorry about that), but it's that you look like you care about the criticism. I mean, when I look at your eyes in these photos and at your body language, you don't look confident now; you look like you're bracing yourself for some impending onslaught of criticism. Like I said, I have no idea what it's like to be famous and it must be just awful to read those terrible things, but I feel like you've kind of left me and my friends in the lurch. What I mean is that if you, the person we could see had the most confidence in the world, the one who gave us the courage to pull that confidence into ourselves and change our own lives, if you're crushed by having an older face, what hope is there for us?

You're not supposed to do that, you know what I mean? We need you to please not do that. We would really like to still look to you and know that we will have great confidence and attitudes at 55 or 65. Please don't be like everyone else now. We never thought your confidence was based on your looks, like other actresses who are more like beauty queen types. We always thought it was something else that was not dependent on looks at all. Please don't make that untrue. Please don't be like all these other women we see around us who are terrified of looking older, who get fillers and plastic surgery and who let themselves be crushed under a mountain of critical words. We don't want to become what we see around us. We want to stay confident, the way we learned from you, and not become broken just because our faces are older.

So, please, Ms. Darvich. Please bring back your confidence and attitude for us, so we can have that to look forward to when we start looking older. Please keep lighting that path.

Sincerely,
Silvie Williams

29

Maple. 55. Office Manager.

Maple focused on keeping it together. In the lobby, on the long green leather couch. Keep it together. Entertainment magazines and trade papers were scattered on the low burl-wood coffee table in front of her. Maple distracted herself by estimating the diameter of the table. It was a tree stump, about four feet across. It must have been an enormous tree once, its core now rubbed with wood oil to a shimmering chestnut color. The color and finish reminded Maple of a horse she'd seen in the winner's circle at the track once.

Maple looked at the other people there in the lobby, waiting also. Were they all interviewing for this job? Maybe. Or maybe there for other meetings. Two men and two other women. They looked like they were in their 20s. Maple ran a hand underneath her thigh, between her skirt and the couch, trying to smooth the wrinkles she knew would be there when she stood up later. She checked the time; she'd been waiting 15 minutes. Maybe she should leave. She could. Just leave and forget this stupid idea about working again. She shouldn't be here. Everyone at this company was her son's age. Everyone, almost everyone. Her, sitting here so clearly older than the rest, the difference so clearly indicated in her face. They were never going to hire her. This was a stupid idea. Maple was stupid.

"Maple?"

She looked up, surprised. In her mind, she was already at the elevators, pressing the call button, waiting for the doors to open. A woman stood in front of her, by the receptionist's Lucite desk. She was about 45 or so. Jeans and heels, silver necklaces.

"Hi, I'm Frances. C'mon back." Frances tilted her head down the hall and Maple stood. As she followed the woman, Maple self-consciously shook the back of her skirt a bit, to cancel the wrinkles she was sure the other, still-seated candidates had seen.

"Here we are." They sat on matching beige vinyl armchairs in a small conference room. "I like to do the interviews in here," Frances started. "Don't need to have a desk between us for our first meeting!"

"I like your necklaces."

Frances touched the chains at her throat. "Oh, thank you. I got them in Santa Fe . . . I love your skirt."

"Oh! I was trying to smooth the wrinkles out before anyone noticed," Maple laughed. "I can't do anything about the wrinkles on my face, but I can at least help my clothes . . ."

"Well, I'm glad to finally meet you."

"I'm very happy to be here. I love the style of the place."

"It's not big-time, like some of the places you've worked, but we're excited to be on the forefront of what's happening in sports equipment now."

Maple smiled, self-conscious still. Self-conscious.

Frances looked down at Maple's résumé, "I mean, IBM, NordickTrack, Adidas . . . You've really got the kind of experience in an office manager that we need. Someone who knows this world . . ."

"Oh, that was so long ago . . ." Maple waved her hand vaguely.

Frances paused and then referred to her résumé again. "And you were once on the city council? Who doesn't want city contacts when it comes to zoning and permits and all that?"

"Yes, some of my friends are still there . . ."

"Well, confidentially, we are thinking about expanding into a building we're hoping to buy, so those contacts would be well appreciated."

Maple adjusted herself in her seat and straightened her blouse. "That is, if those friends are still alive," she joked.

Frances put the résumé down in her lap. "Maple, tell me what brought you back to the workforce. I assume the gap in employment was for raising kids?"

"Yes, that's correct. I was working while they were small, but then my son got into competitive swimming and my daughter wound up on a traveling robotics team and it was just impossible for my husband and me to both keep working. My husband had just gotten a promotion, so it was just easier for me to shift to my new life as the kids' chauffeur!" Maple laughed.

"Sounds like you continued your career of coordinating and organizing a lot of activity, with everything your kids had going on."

Maple blinked. "Oh, you're right. Yeah, I guess I did."

"So your kids are in college now?"

"Yes, my son's at Northwestern and my daughter is headed to Columbia."

"So you're getting back to work. That's exciting."

"Well, I look ancient now, so we'll see about that."

Frances folded her arms, leaned back into the armchair, and looked at Maple for a moment. "Why are you doing that?"

"Pardon?"

"We've been talking for just five minutes and you've made at least three references to looking older."

Maple didn't know what to say, what to do. Her mouth slightly agape, she sat there, hoping some options would quickly enter her brain.

"I work in HR, and an older-looking face is actually something we try to not bring up. We believe that our candidates should be considered on their experience and merit and not on how they look."

"I'm . . . I'm sorry."

Frances reached out and touched Maple's knee briefly. "It's OK. I just find it ironic that you're doing it to yourself."

"I'm . . . I don't know what to say." Tears stung Maple's eyes and she concentrated on not letting them fall over the bottom rim of her eyelashes.

"Well, we think you're the best candidate who applied."

"I'm sorry . . . I didn't realize I was doing that. I guess I was . . . I just . . . I haven't done anything, you know, on my face, to fix it, and I just assumed that my face would make people think I couldn't do the job, or . . ."

"It's like you were trying to fire yourself before you even got the job."

Maple smiled carefully. "Yeah, I guess."

"Well, hiring and firing is *my* job," Frances joked. "Don't take my job, OK?" Maple laughed with her. "Hey, I don't look 20 either, but you can't pay attention to that. You've got to look at your worth, because that's what other people are looking at too."

Maple nodded, a bit more composed.

"We'd like to offer you the job. Could you come work for us?"

Maple grinned. "Really? Oh, thank you!"

Frances and Maple stood and shook hands. Frances was saying something about e-mailing Maple new-hire paperwork and starting in a week. Maple nodded and said her goodbyes as she made her way back through the lobby, past the enormous tree-trunk coffee table, and out to the elevators. Maple pushed the call button and looked at herself in the chrome elevator doors as she waited. She smiled at herself, in triumph, and saw her age in the polished surface: the wrinkles on her face and on her skirt. She forced herself to keep smiling as the elevator doors opened, and prayed she wouldn't talk herself out of this job.

30

Lindsay. 49. College Undergrad.

The lecture hall was cold again, of course. It didn't seem to matter what the temperature was outside, this hall's thermostat appeared to be firmly set at 60 degrees. Lindsay pulled a sweater over her head and flipped her ponytail out of the neck. Now in her sophomore year at school after coming back, she knew to keep a sweater jammed down in the bottom of her backpack for these inexplicably cold lecture halls. She took out her notebook and a pen from her backpack and slouched down in the scratchy wool upholstered seat, knees against the seat back in front of her.

Early in the quarter, just the second lecture of this course, really. Sociology and Evolution, a prereq for some other class Lindsay wanted to take. The professor was a little boring, but she liked the topic. She was fascinated by societal behavior, the agreements we have with each other and all that. It was crowded, 250 students: a necessary feeder class for a few upper-level sociology courses.

Lindsay took notes, was half-paying attention (which she knew she shouldn't do, but she always had the readings to fall back on), when she thought she heard the professor say something about older women's faces and "an indicator of a lack of fertility and is therefore undesired." She sat up a bit and looked sideways at her seatmate's notes, to see if she'd written down what Lindsay thought the professor had just said from the podium. It was there. Her classmate had underlined "undesired" twice, using the red option from her four-color Bic pen. Lindsay looked at the professor, at the front, reading from his notes, sometimes, and then not.

"Evolution dictates that adult men are the center of society, and so everyone else's status is relative to how it serves that group."

Lindsay reluctantly wrote this down. After all, it could wind up on the midterm.

"When a female is of childbearing age, especially in the first half of that childbearing window, she can have anything she wants from a dominant male society, but once age shows on her face—wrinkles, saggy skin, jowls—she will be ignored."

Lindsay looked around to see if any of her young female classmates were annoyed by this guy.

"And rightly so; she is no longer of use to that male-dominated society."

Lindsay squinted, tilted her head to the side, and muttered "What?" under her breath.

"Let's say a woman is older, and attractive, or was once attractive, has kept in good shape, is healthy, nice personality, intelligent, good sense of humor, but has bags under her eyes, loose skin on her neck, etc. . . . . The males no longer need her or want her around, and the younger females reject her for fear of being included *with* her."

Lindsay, at 49 with wrinkles and a bit of loose skin on her neck and the beginnings of bags under her eyes, raised her hand. "Professor, are you referring to the tribal behavior of early man? And of *all* tribes? Or is this just confined to one continent or another? Just to what era are you referring?"

The professor strained his eyes to see Lindsay, sitting in the middle of the large auditorium. "This is . . . There's no era constraint to these findings." He then turned a page in his notes, to continue the lecture.

"But . . . excuse me . . . what are you basing this on? What are the findings, exactly?" Lindsay's voice rose a bit.

"You see women talking about this on *Oprah* all the time," he announced dismissively.

Lindsay could hear her classmates shifting in their seats. Maybe glad she was saying something, or maybe wanting her to just shut up so they could continue taking notes.

"I mean no disrespect, but are you basing this on scientific data, or on things said by Oprah's guests? Because I'm 49 and my friends and I have wrinkles and loose skin and none of what you're saying is true for us. We're not dismissed and forgotten, and we have plenty of acceptance by adult males . . . I would hate to think that any of the 19-year-old women in here are now going to be frightened about getting older, and that they are going to be abandoned as soon as their faces aren't smooth . . . It's just not true."

"Well, the data is overwhelming," the professor distractedly responded.

"What data?" Lindsay sat there waiting for him to reference some study, some anthropological white paper, some peer-reviewed article, but he didn't. He didn't use slides; there were no charts, no pie graphs. He wasn't referencing any of the required readings; he just had his pile of stapled notes. And the professor was done with Lindsay's questions. He was already intently looking at this notes to find the spot where he left off, before she'd interrupted him.

After a moment, Lindsay sat back in her seat. She'd already had more than a couple of professors stick stubbornly to their lecture script, in spite of the existence of evidence to the contrary, so he wasn't unusual. She really hoped that what he'd said hadn't gone into the young women all around her in the auditorium and planted itself, like some dormant flower bulb, patiently waiting to blossom and poison their psyche in 20 years. She hoped it had instead gone through one ear and out the other. Or she hoped that what she'd said to him had canceled any young students' inclination to take anything this professor was saying as fact.

She also hoped it was still early enough in the quarter to drop this class.

31

Gloria. 89. Dead.

One square foot. That's what Gloria figured it measured. One square foot. She had bought shirts and tablecloths and baby blankets and bedsheets and fabric for curtains, and so many yards of fabric, so many square feet, and none of them much mattered. One square foot? What was that? Something just big enough to place a pair of shoes on. Something you could rest a bowling ball upon. Nothing.

Standing there (or hovering? floating? drifting? She couldn't tell), looking at her face. They had made it up. Nice, she supposed, but not really her style. Too much blush. Standing there, looking at her face. One square foot, really, of skin. That's all it really was. Nothing. And yet, it had dominated her life. So much of it. One square foot.

It seemed so bizarre to Gloria now. So positively foreign. She almost couldn't relate to it at all. She could remember, though, could remember being consumed with it. She couldn't remember why. One square foot of skin had demanded her attention almost always. Had dictated her mood every day, had ruined her time alive, really. One square foot. Not the

larger piece of skin on her arms or legs. Not the relatively enormous cylinder of skin on her back and
chest. Just what was on her face, just the top of the
bag of skin in which her bones and organs and nerves
and brain were held. Just the top. Nothing else.

She remembered being paralyzed by it, by how
it looked, how it would be perceived, how she might
be treated as a result of its condition, its arrangement. A mood ring, really; the day's mood predicated
on others' reaction of it. Buoyed up by any compliment on its tone or color when she was younger.
"Glowing." "Radiant." "So pretty today." And then,
for most of her life, unhappy. So unhappy because
of a lack of those comments. A slide away from that.
A long, increasingly dark period of worry. Worry that
it wasn't right anymore, that *she* wasn't right anymore, that her only admission ticket into happiness,
into what made people happy to see her, was continuously disintegrating. Everything else in her life
was fine, was expanding, she supposed, was good
and fine, but that square foot of skin was shifting
like sand, a long overnight blowing of sand off the
beach and into the ocean. Changed while the beach
hotel guests slept. Then, them slipping down to the
shoreline in the early morning to claim their beach
chairs and noticing, "Hey, the beach looks different."
It was something like that, something you could do
nothing about, something that happened while you
were out, asleep, not paying attention. Something

that changed. She remembered now how her face had dominated her thoughts, all of them, really. So much time spent.

She suddenly stopped thinking about it. She instead looked at her daughter and son, her grandson, her husband, in the first and second rows, in front of the casket. She didn't feel sad, just marveled at their movements, their lives, the smells she knew they were smelling, the food they would taste at the wake, the baths they may take later. The books they would now read, the movies they'd see, the triumphs they'd experience. She wanted to touch all that suddenly. Wanted to put it on like a large animal pelt, a bear skin, maybe, and then lie down on the ground and roll around in it. Cherry blossom trees and strawberry jam and knitting and car races and mathematical equations, rocket launches, jazz music. She wanted to gather it all between herself and the bear-skin pelt and then pull the pelt close like a burrito or a cocoon so that all of that would soak into her, the way it hadn't when she was alive. The way it hadn't then.

Her girlfriends were there, four rows back. Sitting together, old like her. Huddled together, one scared, one resigned, one bitter. Huddled together like birds in a zoo. Half aware of their unique qualities, the ones that had caused their selection for this zoo, and also fully aware of the distractingly restrictive qualities of their surroundings, something that did not at all match the place from whence they'd been snatched. Too painful. Gloria knew they felt their faces remained on them like a copy of a copy of a copy of the original image. Corroded from the inside with disappointment and disbelief that the world had stopped being impressed by their one square foot of skin. And so early too. Before 40, for most of them.

Gloria turned away. So much lost time. She couldn't look at people, her friends, anyone, still doing it, still in the throes of that obsession with their face. So much authority turned over, absolutely turned over to others. Why had Gloria done it? So much time lost. So many opportunities not taken, so many happy moments left unredeemed, like lottery tickets left in a drawer. She could almost touch the sorrow over that; she could see it resting there, as a glowing bundle nearby. Close enough to touch if she wanted, but far enough to justify the choice of simply watching it dissolve. She wanted to touch it, though, just a bit, like wanting to feel the labor pains before the epidural is injected. Just a touch. She reached out and felt a piercing through her spirit, like a cleaver into a coconut, splitting the hard shell and meat, and releasing the water inside. She withdrew her hand quickly, resolved now to just watch it disappear instead, a tidy bag of ash from a furnace of self-loathing and voluntary exclusion from life. She was glad to watch it go and was relieved to never again have to think of things like that. To have other experiences now, she assumed, unrelated to society and the limitations within that.

What a funny thing it was, though, to have let that one foot square of skin distract her so utterly from the experiences of her life.

32

Bertie. 37. Patternmaker.

The skin on Bertie's face was thirsty for the sun. It drank it like a street cat sucks milk from a Good Samaritan's bowl. She tilted her head to absorb the sun's glare more squarely, and still her face, the skin on her face, wanted more. She'd been early to meet her friend, her sometimes friend, who often showed up, but not always. She was early to be in the good weather, a day that convinces you that the circle of life never ends with death. The first day that really felt like spring, where the daffodils on the street, the bulbs that brownstone owners had buried months before, where the daffodils were no longer surrounded by the mortifying reminder of winter, not pushing against the last ice crystals atop decayed leaves that had been paralyzed under the first snow, months ago. The first day where the daffodils were free of any of that. The sun fresh and the spring air taking stage as itself. Not as a momentary respite from winter, and not as an understudy of summer, but spring fully, and completely, starring itself.

She knew she had a good 30 minutes. (At least. Who knew if her friend would actually show up. Bertie was half-certain she'd get a text saying her friend had overslept or some other sophomoric shit.) The park, near the restaurant, that bench. She took out her book and broke the spine. Very satisfying. Could only happen once per book, and she loved it every time. She broke the spine and looked up, distracted by the old apartment building in front of her. The book lay in her lap, sprawled, like an available woman who was unaware of her options. Bertie looked up at that building and marveled at the grand entrance, the gargoyles, the marble lobby. She guessed (correctly, she was sure) that the building was full of longtime tenants, loathe to ever move out. She guessed (rightly so, she was sure) that the only way anyone ever got an apartment in that building was if someone died. Oh, and you had to be quick. Yes. You'd have to be right on it. Scanning the obituaries, she was sure, for the names you had researched beforehand, of the people who lived there. Quick, and snap the apartments up. Then, snuggle in and never move. You didn't move from a building like that in New York City, no.

Bertie wondered if any of the old people were ever pushed to the edge. If they were ever convinced by those who wanted their apartments that they should get out, go to an old folks home, or just die. Bertie self-consciously touched her face. Would someone younger look at her someday and ignorantly assume she was headed in that direction? If Bertie was living in that building, would others, younger ones, look at her face then and start estimating the length of time they'd have to wait for her apartment? And would plastic surgery change that? If she had plastic surgery, would that scare them off? Would that say to them, "Hey, not this one. This one's here to stay, this one's not about to go. This one is young, so back the fuck off." Would plastic surgery say that?

Bertie tilted her head and imagined old people being flung off the roof of the building, like in the Viking era. Take the old people to the cliff, whatever cliff you had designated as the place to get rid of the old. Take them to the cliff and tell them to jump, or just toss them over. This was a rumor, sure, about that era, but it wasn't exactly out of character for the Vikings, based on what Bertie had read. The old ones as a drain and a burden on the community: the old could not fight or farm, and just sucked the tribe of resources. Like a child, but without the promise of future strength and future babies. Just a child, but weak and impotent. Yes, invited to jump, or tossed off the cliff. Bertie thought of others, the Eskimos. Moving away in the dead of night, not waking the oldest of them, leaving them there to starve and die on the ice. A drain on the tribe. Impossible to keep them on.

We're not the Vikings. Or the Eskimos. And maybe all rumors anyway. Bertie knew that. But, she wondered how much of this was coded in our evolutionary seeds. How many people, if they could, would line up the older-looking people in the building and walk them up the back stairs, to the roof, and use some kind of switch or broom to bat them off the rooftop in order to get their apartments.

Bertie wondered if an older face was treated like the red crystal in the film *Logan's Run*. Yes, of course. In the film, the hand crystal turning red meant you were now too old for society. No longer useful, and in need of being killed. That's the circle of life, some would argue. Of course, it's only those who are nowhere near the end of that cycle who argue the veracity of the theory. Bertie thought the circle of life must be rather something like the endless repetition of the seasons. Where spring always, always follows winter. And an older face can belie some clever means by which the less-clever youth will never get that fantastic apartment.

33

Diane. 39. Schoolteacher.

Diane felt like crying and screaming at the same time. Her face in her hands. Tears through the fingertips. Almost. Breathing. Breathe in and out, but involuntarily. (This isn't a damn yoga retreat.) Frustration, looking for relief, a way out down a river of breath.

What had she done with her life? What had she fucking done? Taught children, fine, but what was that? And how could she rid herself of this seemingly limitless burden of incompletion? Every day that passed, every day, she felt it. This engine, this shame, SHAME, for not accomplishing something, anything it seems, something worthy, worthwhile, something to be acknowledged every fucking day. Something ALL PEOPLE would stand up and see and applaud and acknowledge as worthwhile. Every day.

Where was that? That was a problem, that Diane thought that way. Yes. That was a problem. Her face exacerbated it. Made it worse. She actually didn't care that she was looking older, didn't care, really. Loved seeing older faces on actresses, when she went to the movies or watched TV. Loved it. But all those actresses could look ancient and it would be fine. They could say they'd earned it, that they'd achieved the important goals, so it doesn't matter. Their faces, it doesn't matter.

Diane couldn't look in the mirror lately. For a while now. Her smile lines and gray streak (just at the right temple) reminded her that she was still making the salary of a college intern, really. It reminded her that though it's normal for people in their 30s to own a house, she didn't see how she could ever afford that. Reminded her that she had decided not to have kids, and that she was a couple of years away from never being able to amend that decision.

She couldn't really look in a mirror now. It was just getting worse. It would never get better. Her own face (and hair) mocking her lack of accomplishment. It would always get worse.

34

Amy. 19. College Student.

INT. FAMILY HOME-DINING ROOM-EARLY EVENING

AMY, 19, is having dinner with her father, STEVE, early 50s, and her brother, DANE, 23. A TV can be heard in the next room.

Steve has gauze and an ice pack around his face. Amy is flipping through a magazine.

> STEVE
> (re: a photo in the
> magazine)
>She's gross.

> AMY
>She's OK. I like her.

> DANE
>She was hot in *Carjack II*.

> STEVE
>She's gross. Look at that
>plastic surgery.

                          AMY
                  (frowning)
          What?

                                      CROSS DISOLVE

INT. RESTAURANT-DAY-FLASHBACK

*Amy, Steve, and Amy's mother, SUE, early
50s, sit at a restaurant booth, as a WOMAN,
late 40s, walks by.*

                      STEVE
                  *(re: the woman's
                    face)*
          That woman's gross. Bad nose job.

INT. FAMILY HOME-LIVING ROOM-NIGHT-FLASHBACK

*Steve and Amy sit before the TV. Steve is
seated on the couch and Amy is seated on the
floor, doing her homework on the coffee table.*

                      STEVE
                  *(re: the actress on
                    the TV)*
          That woman's gross.

Amy rolls her eyes.

EXT. BEACH-DAY-FLASHBACK

A younger Amy and TWO GIRLFRIENDS sit on a
large blanket, talking. An empty chair is
nearby. TWO WOMEN, late 40s, talk nearby.

Steve approaches Amy and the girlfriends
with cold, newly purchased drinks.

> STEVE
> (as he hands them
> drinks, re: one of
> the two women)
> That woman's gross. Bad boob job.

Amy gets up and signals her girlfriends
to follow her to the shore.

INT. FRIEND'S HOME-ENTRANCEWAY-NIGHT-
FLASHBACK

Steve, Sue, Amy, and Dane have just arrived to a holiday party. They hand their
coats over to the hostess.

> STEVE
> (sotto voce to Sue,
> re: one of the
> guests)
> That woman's gross. Bad
> face-lift.

Sue shakes her head for him to be quiet.

INT. FAMILY HOME-DINING ROOM-EARLY EVENING-
CONTINUOUS

Amy continues to look at Steve.

> STEVE
> (re: the woman in the
> magazine)
> It's gross.

> AMY
> Oh, but you literally just
> spent tens of thousands of
> dollars and went through this
> whole procedure with your eyes
> and your neck.

Dane chokes back a laugh.

STEVE

Well, I had to do it, because
I looked gross.

Amy gives Steve a quizzical look.

STEVE (CONT'D)

I was doing the world a ser-
vice by having the plastic
surgery. It's OK for me, but
it's not OK for other people.

AMY

God, Dad. You're so dumb.

CUT TO BLACK

35

Tory. 53. Writer.

Her face was older.

Her skin was looser, less fat filling it out; it creased more easily.

She felt ashamed. Every time she spoke to people.

She knew that was wrong. Irrational.

Feeling exposed when deliverymen or workmen came to the house. Always wearing sunglasses to greet them. Always.

Wouldn't they treat her the same without them? Perhaps. Perhaps.

Sunglasses to put an intermediary between Tory and the deliveryman's opinion. Retard his ability to form an opinion. Obscure it.

Tory's face didn't really bother her. Strangely.

She liked it, really. She liked it.

She wasn't always ashamed. It had started somewhere.

She thought.

When she'd heard some women in a bookstore, ten years ago, talking about her author photo, inside the flap.

Tory slipping into a bookstore and lurking near her books, there on the shelf, to hear what the people said.

Years ago. The shame was that old. Ten years ago.

Surprised. Surprised. "Oh wow. She aged."

Tory hadn't. Not really. Not much at all.

Then the other woman. "Jesus. I'm the same age as her and she looks 20 years older."

Tory didn't. She didn't.

But Tory felt shame fertilize her ego, and then felt it divide and subdivide and multiply, and then its sections separate and disperse throughout her.

That was a long time ago, but Tory still fed it, those sections now corroding her system.

Needed to edit that memory. Tory would do that. Pretend the women had said she looked great, and expel the memory's fertilized egg. Abort it, really.

She changed it, Tory changed it, pretended something else was said by the women. Ran it through her head.

But, there was something else. It wasn't the face. It wasn't the face.

If the women were to have never said that . . .

It was that they were saying *anything* disparaging of Tory. That was what hit her. (In the middle of the upper back, where the horror-film killer stabs you. Where you can't reach around and take the knife out.)

It was that they *thought they could talk that way about Tory*.

She had written four books at that point, two of them *New York Times* Best Sellers. Part of "30 Under 30 to Watch" back then, and all that. "Breathtaking work," and all that.

She hadn't written a best seller in a few years. That's fine. Tory knew that. How could she not?

But the women were speaking so disrespectfully, as if they were up there, up high, and Tory was no longer revered. Not even at their level now, but beneath. Yanked down from her ones-to-watch level, her cloud, her platform of respect, and flung to the ground, beneath the ground. To be reviled, spat at, buried alive.

That's what the women did, really. Buried Tory alive.

Her face was emblematic of her lack of work. To Tory. That's what she had done, how her head had let those comments, those attitudes, fertilize her ego. Like that.

It wasn't her older face she was ashamed of, it was that her older face was emblematic of her lack of work.

She was writing still. Of course. Of course, writing rich and meaningful work. But not the kind of work that once blew wind up those women's skirts. Not what the women could superficially absorb. So, Tory was dirt now. To them. To them, she was dirt.

The women had to put her there on the ground, beneath the ground, because the other, more recent writing Tory was doing, the women couldn't understand that. They could only understand, would only try to understand (the laziness, the inability), the writing which many others, many, many others had lifted up, lauded and seen, in the most populist ways, in the most superficial ways.

So Tory had conflated the shame of being seen as a failure, a damn disappointment, in these women's eyes, with having an older face.

And didn't know it. For ten years. Tory didn't know it.

36

Rose. 42. Baker.

Flowers, flowers everywhere. Oh, that thrilled Rose.
Even her name would tell you her love of flowers.
On the coffee table, on the dining room table, in the
niche in the painted cinder-block wall. In the bathrooms, in the kitchen, the bedroom, the guest room
(when someone's expected). Everywhere. Flowers
outside as well, yes. Roses (yes) of all colors, not
just one or two, like some houses. Dusky purple, soft
peach, butter yellow, pure white, deep red, ballet
pink, creamy orange. Lilac flowers too, on the bush,
in the spring only. What a lovely smell. Always.
Gladiolas and bearded irises, even the black ones
Rose ordered special online from Holland. Flowers
everywhere.

Rose dressed that way too, like a flower. Chiffon was a favorite material, in colorful hues, opaque
through many layers, sheer through a few, and a hint
of color with only one layer. Beautiful, like a flower.

She was on her way out for the night. A party.
One she'd been looking forward to for a while. An
engagement party of a friend in the old Rolland Ballroom on the east side of town. That one. So beautiful.

Raspberry chiffon dress with blackberry tulle underneath was tonight's choice. Rose's mother's costume jewelry in the palm of her hand, to place on her ears. Rose's boyfriend was minutes away, to pick her up, to bring her to the party. Rose slipped on her satin slides and moved to the big mirror in the entrance hall, near her front door. Her dress virtually floating before her and behind her. Earrings in hand.

Before the mirror. One earring on the delicate ledge under the mirror. One yellow costume-jeweled earring between her fingers.

And look. Look in the mirror. Look in the mirror, Rose. Yes, put that earring into the little hole in your left earlobe. Place it in and look at yourself, Rose. Look hard. Get the back of it on, so the earring doesn't fall out tonight at the Rolland Ballroom, on the dance floor. Is it in? Secure? Look at it in the mirror. Look at yourself. Are you looking? Are you looking hard, Rose? Because there are issues. There are fucking issues. The dress, fine, the earrings will do, but look, Rose, look at your face. Are you looking? Looking hard? Because you need to. There are problems, with your eyes. Problems. Don't you think someone will notice the way those creases break all the way across you face, under your eye, when you smile? Someone will most certainly notice that. The forehead, with the three distinct horizontal lines, like ruled notebook paper. Someone will most certainly take note of that. The lines around your mouth, the vertical smoker's lines, though you've never smoked, still, inexplicably, they are there, and they will be noticed. Most certainly.

Turn your face, Rose, and look at the profile. Turn as far as you can to the side, so you can see what others will notice when you aren't paying attention. The neck will be noticed. Not as bad as it will become later, but bad now, nonetheless. The neck muscles have protruded greatly over the last year. A trend, to be sure. People will notice that tonight.

Truly, Rose, I don't know how you can be seen in this state, the state of you. Of being you, of having this face that most people, all people, perhaps, will most certainly notice is flawed. Is that the doorbell? Is your boyfriend here? I suppose you need to leave now. You'll need to hate what we discussed. You'll need to hate it before the others can. Hate it for them. That's the only way to escape the criticism that will surely come tonight. Hate your face before they can.

Rose called out to her boyfriend, "Be right there!" Her hand trembling, just a bit, inserting the post for the other earring, pushing the back on. She looked in the mirror once again, and couldn't see herself anymore. She could see her dress, her beautiful dress. She could see the flowers behind her, on the table in the dining room, and beyond, in the kitchen. But she couldn't see her face anymore. She couldn't see her face.

"Be right there!"

37

Laura. 52. Actress.

Laura always had to downplay the importance of these network TV "test" auditions. Sure, the producers had narrowed down the candidates to just two or three actresses, and sure, whoever got the job was looking at a potential money and exposure explosion, but you couldn't think about any of that. Laura couldn't; it would have utterly derailed her focus on the audition.

Sitting in the lobby, in a gray upholstered armchair, Laura had to think about something else, she knew. At least this role was a character who was over 50. Laura had stopped auditioning for roles younger than herself a few years ago. First, it was just the "This role's not quite for me" to her agent, but after a while, she finally just told her agent not to send her any under-50 parts. Laura thought her agency might just drop her, not represent her anymore, but it worked out OK. She just couldn't stand not looking her age anymore. She didn't want to look younger; she just wanted to look the way she looked.

"Can I get you a water? Anything?" from the producer's assistant.

Laura smiled, "Oh no, thank you. I'm fine."

"Sorry to make you wait." The assistant turned to get back to the audition room, at the end of the hall, where another actress was reading for a wall of network TV executives.

In her early 40s, Laura had still auditioned for any character in their late 20s or 30s. She seemed to pass for that range without a problem, had prided herself on that, even. Yes, until that one job. Laura didn't remember how old that character was supposed to be. And did that matter anyway? The age was just some number the writer throws out there, on the paper. It shouldn't have mattered.

But, that one job, something with horses or dogs. They were lighting Laura all wrong. Not lighting correctly for even someone with a young and perfect bone structure. Laura thought maybe it was going OK, that those lines around her mouth and those shadows under her eyes were OK here. Maybe they didn't look so bad. Maybe Laura had been succumbing to some broken-mirror syndrome when she saw those flaws under this light. She was only half-conscious of it midway through the shoot (after all, no one had said anything), when the director took her aside during their lunch break.

"Can I talk to you?"

"Sure!" Laura followed the director imagining this would be about the character or scheduling or waiving overtime, something. The director stopped when they were far enough from the crew to not be heard. He took a breath and looked Laura in the face. She wondered if she was about to be fired.

"Laura . . . are you all right?"

She raised her eyebrows and tried to remember if she'd behaved on the set in some way for which she needed to apologize. She couldn't think of anything.

"Yeah, I'm fine. Why?" Laura smiling, with just enough incredulity on her face.

"Are you being abused?" from the director. Then, "Because your face . . ."

Goddamnit. The fucking lighting. The lighting was so damn bad on this film. She knew it. Laura knew it. They just hadn't been saying anything, hadn't corrected the bad lighting, maybe even didn't know *how* to fix the bad lighting, and instead just assumed that Laura was abused. That she looked so unattractive under this lighting, her 42-year-old face for this 35-year-old character, or whatever, that they assumed she'd been bashed about the head, that she'd been regularly abused, punched in the face, yeah. Christ. Laura wanted to say, "I know! My face. It's not great, I'm looking older too. I know, but if you could just light it correctly, we'd all be fine." Laura so badly wanted to tell this director that it was this godawful lighting, but the cinematographer was some old friend of his, some "creative brother," he called him. Some guy who'd won an Emmy a thousand years ago, who everyone said was great, but who Laura saw didn't know what he was doing and lit women so they looked like someone had bashed their faces in.

"Laura, we're ready." The producer's assistant was there again, in the lobby. Laura stood and picked up her purse.

The other actress, now done with her audition, was walking through the lobby on her way out. She whispered a "Good luck!" to Laura as she passed by. Laura smiled back. Another "older-looking" actress for this network TV test. That felt right.

After that "face abuse" experience, Laura had gone through the compulsive checking with cinematographers on film and TV show jobs that followed, making sure that they were adjusting for the shadow her forehead made over her eyes, for the mouth creases, all of it. And Laura, doing what she could, tilting her head just right when she was on-camera, micromanaging the makeup artists, until it got to such a point that Laura could barely focus on her own job of playing the character. Until she wound up on her mom's couch in Seattle, crying for three days and not knowing how to stop. That was when Laura stopped auditioning for any character younger than herself. It was then. She couldn't take it anymore. And she didn't care what that meant: her own agent possibly dropping her, or never working again. It couldn't matter anymore; she couldn't stop how she looked. It was all too much.

Laura walked into the network audition, a conference room with a single chair (hers) on one side and a couch and 10 chairs (theirs) on the other side. The wall of 13 executives and producers seated there all gave a hearty hello and Laura sat down in her chair to begin the audition for the part of a 55-year-old law professor; someone who looked just like her.

38

Frankie. 55. Engineer.

Green leaves. And a bird. A wren? A robin? Frankie used to know this better. Her bird-watching book was probably still in the house, in the bookcase under the stairs. Her parents never threw out books, so she was sure it was still there.

The sounds up here! The air! The lake lapped at the small, sharp rocks that lined the shore. The rocks that made her and her brothers wear their old canvas basketball sneakers to step into the water. Every time, every year. Shivering with the anticipation of the icy water smearing itself over their limbs, and wiping the sweat of the summer's day from them.

"Frankie!" Her mother, hobbling—damnit, was she hobbling?—out the front door, coming down off the wood porch to help Frankie—no, probably just to watch Frankie pull her bags out of the back of her car. That was OK, Frankie's mother was older; it was OK.

"Mama. Hello!" Frankie freed her duffel bag and her tennis racquet from her car's hatchback before slamming it closed. "Is Darren here yet? Or Benny? He here?"

They hugged and Frankie's mother patted Frankie on the back of the neck, the way she always did. "Darren's here with the kids . . ."

They walked into the wood-shingled house, Frankie inhaling deeply before entering, as if to capture the trees and the sounds of the birds and the filtered light, and pull it all into the house with her.

"Hey!" from Darren, and little hugs from his little kids.

Frankie then hugged Darren as the kids ran out toward the lake. "Thank God they still hug me. Nina is SO over that."

Darren smiled and pointed down the hall. "Ellen can't come until Sunday, so you get your own room this time."

"Dad fishing?"

"You know what you're having for dinner."

Frankie winked and walked down the hall and up the stairs to her room. She called it "her room," the far corner room where you could see the big pine up where the owl's nest used to be. The room looked the same, pretty much, as when they used to come up every other weekend as kids. Green wool bedspread, powder-blue eyelet curtains on the windows over the bed. Frankie could now hear her other brother, Benny, laughing downstairs. She dropped her bag on the bed and went to greet him.

Bigger, bigger than she last saw him. Not fatter, bigger. His flannel-shirted back to her as she came down the hall. Beyond him was Darren again, an eager look on his face now and a young woman she didn't know.

"Benny!"

He spun around. "Frankie. What is this jacket you have on? I'm going to get you one of my shirts."

"Oh my God, I don't want one of your shirts. Sleeping-bag size."

"No, I brought one in your size from the warehouse. I'll get it later." Benny turned and held an arm out to the young woman, the one Frankie didn't know. "So, you were busy and couldn't meet Jenny when we were in town last . . ." He tucked the petite blonde under his shoulder. Jenny smiled.

Frankie reached out and touched Jenny's forearm. "It's great to meet you. Welcome! I hope Benny braced you for the Davis family fish festival tonight . . ."

Jenny looked up at Benny. "Oh yeah. Benny told me your dad does this for his birthday every year."

"Who wants a drink? I need a drink!" Darren turned to Jenny, especially to Jenny. "I make a great margarita. You want a margarita?" Attentive.

Frankie made a face. Just a little one.

Jenny nodded, "Sure!" And Darren quickly scooted to the kitchen.

Frankie turned and yelled toward the kitchen pass-through, "Uh . . . I'll have one too, Darren."

"Oh yeah, sure!" he tossed from the other side of the wall, his head deep in the fridge, scanning for limes.

"Benny? The bathroom?" Jenny looked down the hall.

"Yeah, third door on the right." And Jenny went.

Benny moved to the pass-through counter and sat down on one of the stools. "So, what do you think?" to Darren in the kitchen, to Frankie walking over and sitting on a stool herself.

"Fuuuuck, Benny. You gotta ask? She's flawless. Man, is she 18, or . . ."

"23. Relax."

"Wow, Benny." Frankie was already looking at herself in the reflection in the polished stainless steel over the stove, behind Benny and his margarita making, there at the kitchen counter. Not conscious yet, not consciously looking at her age.

"Get over it."

"Oh, I'm over it. All over it. Jesus, Benny. She's perfect." Darren quickly cutting up the small limes.

"Of course she looks perfect. She's barely out of the womb. Her skin's seen maybe four summers' worth of sun . . ."

"Frankie, you're 55. Back off the comparing."

"She's beautiful, Benny, that's all." Darren taking a pull of tequila from the bottle.

"Listen, I want to tell you before she comes back." Benny looked over his shoulder, then back at them. "I'm going to ask her to marry me at dinner."

"Oh, man." Darren grinned and mock-panted.

"What is the matter with you?" Frankie squinted

at Darren. "So, Ellen will be here Sunday?" she threw at him.

Darren gave her a look and poured the margarita mix into three glasses. He paused and looked up at Frankie. "Oh . . . did you want one?"

The mosquitoes weren't out yet, even at dusk; it was too early in the season. The old wooden picnic table in the backyard, between the house and the lake. The thick pillar candles; the carcasses of the five trout Frankie's father had caught and cleaned and pan-fried.

Attentive, her father had been attentive to Jenny too. Excited. Interested. "When are you going to put a baby in there?!" and other things older men know they shouldn't say, but know they can get away with saying. Frankie wasn't going to be jealous about this attention to Jenny. Wasn't going to be anything but supportive of her future sister-in-law. But the "Would you like the last fish?" and "Let me give you the last of the tequila . . ." (because none of *us* wanted the last margarita, Darren) made Frankie think about resources, just generally, about who gets them. Jenny, the guest. Jenny, the 23-year-old. Jenny, who doesn't know us much yet, but who will. Jenny, with a flawless face.

Yeah, Frankie was having a problem. With that. Be supportive, be supporting, don't let competitiveness drive a wedge between women. All that. That was in Frankie's head. But also in her head was her last trip to Costa Rica where the tour guide talked about the visual signals the newborn animals, like monkeys, gave their mothers about their health and how the ones looking the healthiest would always be given the most resources. The ones that needed it the least, Frankie remembered thinking. The tour guide had explained, with an accent that made everything sound sure and true, that the mothers fed the ones they thought had the best chance of survival, the flawless ones who appeared to be the best contenders to carry on the lineage.

Frankie excused herself to go to the bathroom, through the screen door, down the hall, third door on the right. The light in the bathroom, in the wood-paneled bathroom, was honey-colored. "Forgiving," she and her friends would joke about that kind of light, now that they're older. Frankie paced a little in the tiny bathroom. Rocked, really, just side to side (there wasn't room to do much more than that), and tried to shake this fear, some fear, that had crept up her back since first meeting Jenny. She finally stopped rocking and stood still. And cried. Quietly, not wanting the sound to carry out the tiny window in the little wood-paneled bathroom, out into the night, where the family sat, smiling at each other, competing with each other to get as many resources to Jenny as possible.

Frankie shook her head. This was ridiculous. She

would have as many resources as before, just as before. She would be taken care of. She would be fine. She splashed water on her face and wiped it off in the mirror with the white hand towel. In the mirror, those wrinkles, those droopy eyelids, they were indicators, to our animal side, that no resources should be spared for her, for Frankie and her old-face indicator. Frankie shook her head a bit again. Don't think about the monkeys, she told herself.

"Hey! Did Mama bring the peaches out yet?" Frankie said brightly, energetically, back at the wooden picnic table. Her mother smiled up at her and pointed to the bowl of roasted peaches. Darren's kids ran on the lawn behind her mother, trying to catch fireflies in empty mayonnaise jars.

Frankie sat down again and swallowed the last of her margarita. Across and down the table, the candlelight was especially flattering on Jenny's face just then. Especially flattering. And Frankie could hear Benny and Darren convincing Jenny to take a large helping of peaches and whipped cream. Frankie furrowed her brow a little as her mother caught her eye. Her mother knew. She knew.

Frankie looked down at the table and whispered to herself, "Don't think about the monkeys."

39

Barbara. 60. Florist.

How was it different?

Barbara's daughter, Fawn, was upset with her, now that Barbara had announced her plans for a face-lift.

"How is this different?" Barbara had asked her.

Every culture has its beauty modifications to make themselves more appealing, more attractive. Tattoos, throughout the ages. On the arms, the legs, the back, the neck and face, even. Piercings, in our ears, our lips, our belly buttons. Lip plates, still practiced by the Mursi tribe, where the bottom lip is cut and increasingly enlarged, accommodating a larger and larger decorative disc.

"This is the same thing," Barbara had insisted, to Fawn. "*They* don't think it's barbaric to stick dinnerware into their faces, so you have no right to judge the plastic surgery I'm going to do. It's no different."

Other practices: tooth sharpening as a rite of passage or a show of status in Mayan culture and in more modern Bali and the Philippines; earlobe discs in the Kenyan Maasai tribe, and the Amazonian Huaorani tribe, and edgy hipsters everywhere. The skull-binding of ancient Peru, Chinese foot binding, and body scarification of West Africa and elsewhere.

How was this any different?

"When you think about it, just cutting some skin and pulling it a tiny bit tighter is far less barbaric than any of that," Barbara had said to Fawn. "Far less barbaric."

And what about circumcision or shaving your legs or dying your hair? How is that any different from plastic surgery? "You're still changing your appearance," from Barbara, to Fawn. "And makeup! How is that any different? When you think about it, how is plastic surgery any different . . . ? It's no different. We're all just getting closer to the beauty ideals of our time."

40

Ellie. 7. First Grader.

The shoes. The shoes were just right. Too cold out-side for them, Ellie's mother had said. Ellie solved the problem with two layers of socks. Ellie's mother called her a "solution finder."

So, sandals, yes, in the fall, in her classroom, with two layers, one thin, one thick, of socks. Red leather flowers on the top and sides of the sandals. Perfect.

Circle time. Ellie grabbed a spot in the cir-cle, near the blue beanbag, and sat down quickly. Criss-cross-applesauce. She shoved her corduroy skirt between her knees, so she could see her san-dals, and grinned up at her teacher, Mrs. Foster.

"Does anyone know what this is?" Mrs. Foster was looking at them all, back and forth.

"Is it invisible?" asked Teddy, from the other side of the circle.

Mrs. Foster put her hands on either side of her head. "This."

Ellie and two or three of her classmates yelled out, "Your face!!"

Mrs. Foster smiled. "That's right. And do you

know what your face can do? Raise your hands this time," she added cheerfully.

Ellie held hers as high as possible, a true touch-the-ceiling attempt.

"Conner?"

"You can smile."

"That's right!"

Another boy, "You can smell!"

"Yes."

Ellie held her raised arm with her other hand.

"Ellie?"

"You can do *this!*" Ellie lifted her eyebrows up and down, up and down.

"Yes, facial expressions. We can show we're happy, sad, frustrated. All of that." A couple of the other children were practicing their best eyebrow raises on each other. "Did you know that we have 43 muscles in our face to make all those expressions and four special muscles on each side, so we can open our mouths really wide and bite an apple or yawn?" The children all opened and closed their mouths. "And all the messages your mouth and your nose and your eyes get are sent right back into your brain, really fast." The children immediately tried to catch the messages, to watch the messages travel from what they were seeing or smelling back into their brains, to catch the journey.

"Isn't it amazing? And no matter what you look like, whether you have blue eyes or brown, or have a round face or a narrow one, or have a young face or an old face, or a light face or a dark face, you get to have all these abilities in your face."

Mrs. Foster noticed Sandy's hand shoot up and nodded to her, encouragingly. "My grandma had a stroking and she can't use part of her face now."

"Oh, Sandy . . . Yes, that's a stroke, where part of your face can get paralyzed, or sort of frozen."

"Yeah, when she smiles now, only half her mouth goes up."

"Well, I hope your grandma feels better really soon . . . We're very lucky to be able to all smile with our whole mouth, right, everyone?" Smiles all around, practicing on each other. "Is there any other part of our outside that does this many things?"

"No!" from the students.

Ellie was feeling her whole face with her hands, while she moved it in different directions.

"Sometimes, there's a problem with a face, and a person needs another face . . . Did you know that doctors can put a new face on someone who needs one?"

"How?" Ellie was amazed.

"It's very complicated, but doctors have to attach all those muscles, so the new face can move; and all those nerves, so the new face can send messages to the brain. It takes a long time, but they can help those people now. Isn't that wonderful?"

The children nodded enthusiastically. Most of

them. The others were looking around for the next item of interest to capture their attention.

"OK, everyone! I think it's snack time . . . Maria, can you open the snack cupboard?"

The children surged toward the back of the room. "Single file!" Mrs. Foster then turned toward her desk for the pile of printed math exercises she would give the children next. Ellie stood nearby.

"Mrs. Foster?"

Mrs. Foster squatted next to Ellie. "Don't you want a snack, sweetie?"

Ellie put her small fingers on the sides of Mrs. Foster's face and traced her smile lines and creases. "Your face works really well, Mrs. Foster. It's a good face."

"Yes, Ellie, I agree. We all have good faces, don't we?"

Ellie nodded and smiled. "Yeah!"

41

Dawn. 58. Sales Executive.

She feared for her, when she saw her. Eight years old or so, green pullover, gray backpack with a cartoon character embroidered on it. On a motorized scooter, in the road, on a busy street. Catching up with her older brothers or some friends, maybe, on her way to school. Dawn wanted to put her on the sidewalk, as she drove past, going the other way. Put the little girl up, out of harm's way. But also knew that the girl, small and defenseless, on a scooter, in the road, would probably be OK. People would look out for her, other drivers, driving up from behind her, going that way on the road. They would look after her. They would get the signal from her small size and her enthusiastic posture, the signal, "This is a little girl, watch out for her, protect her."

Dawn had seen it before, knew everyone had seen it, when dealing with a baby. If a baby was ever left alone, on a doorstep, or on the grass, all alone, people would pick it up, guard it ferociously, even. They would get the signal, looking at the baby face, the small size. That face, that size would signal, "The baby is utterly defenseless, she can do nothing without you."

Dawn knew she did this, read the signals, with other people, of other ages. When she got the fresh batch of interns each year at the office, their youth and ignorance signaled that everyone needed to give them a break, to not expect a particularly strong business savvy yet, to nurture them. And Dawn did that, everyone did that, received the signal "These people need you. They think they know how to do things and they will bring fresh ideas, but they do not know what you know. They need you."

But Dawn couldn't take what she felt her own face signaled now. "This one is over and done, finished, invisible, horrid." That was the signal, Dawn knew. She had tried to intercept that signal with Botox and fillers, she had tried to send a different signal, one that would say, "She's wonderful and worth loving. Take her in, embrace her." Maybe people felt that way toward her anyway, maybe, in spite of her bad signal, and without her constant attempts to change that frequency. Maybe.

Dawn pulled her car into the business park, where her office sat. Past the guard ("Hello, Ms. Miller!"), walked to her building elevator ("Let me get that door for you, Ms. Miller"), to her office ("Morning, Dawn, here's your coffee, and Georgia from Worldwide Marketing is waiting for you in your office . . ."), taking the coffee and sweeping into the first of the day's endless stream of meetings.

And as Dawn sat there, listening to Georgia solicit her approval for the latest marketing campaigns, Dawn had an epiphany.

Her face. Her face didn't signal, "Over and done, finished, invisible, horrid," at all. It signaled authority. It signaled, "This one knows what she's doing. This one can take you through the fire. This one can find the answers." And all her efforts to iron out that signal, the Botox and the fillers, and the upcoming plastic surgery consultation, were all because Dawn was afraid of that authority, afraid that she *didn't* know what she knew, afraid she'd fail to take anyone through the fire, afraid she'd miss the answers.

And then she realized that she *did* know, or she would figure it out, and that there were few people alive who could do it better than her. And she decided to not be afraid anymore.

Her face signaled, "Follow her. She will lead."

42

Jan. 46. Chef.

So much shit. First parent death, a new one for Jan. So many things to sort through in her mom's house, so many papers to file, with the state, with her mother's doctors, her mother's accountants, the hospital. Christ.

Her mother's house had a musty smell. Clean and tidy, but a musty smell in the carpets, something her mother must have gotten used to over the years, used to it so she didn't notice anymore, couldn't smell it anymore. Like people who tar roads or roofs, can't smell that acrid odor anymore. This musty smell was more subtle, obviously, but one more thing to put on the list. Jan would have to shampoo (hopefully not replace) the carpets before she sold the house.

It was a big house. Jan had lived here before moving in with her dad, in middle school. The house had a lot of light, and a pool. Some good moments here, but the thickest memories were of her mother's erratic behavior, around the divorce. Before, during, after. Too much to live with.

Jan couldn't remember if her mother's first face-lift was before or after the divorce, but it had startled her. Her mother had always been very beautiful, like a bird. A stork or a swan, something stately. Jan had even drawn birds at school, when she was small, and given them to her mother. Jan couldn't remember if she ever told her mother they were pictures of her.

Very beautiful, and then the face-lift. It was OK, Jan supposed, but unnecessary. Her mother seemed happy about the face-lift, but that only distracted her a short while. Jan was the last kid home, her older sister already at college, a fair spread in years between them. So, Jan became the focus of her mother's unpredictable behavior. It got easier to deal with her mother after Jan was with her dad, in his smaller place, only 45 minutes away. It was OK. Another school, it was OK.

Jan opened the windows in the hallway, to release the musty carpet smell. She looked out at the pool for a moment and then continued down the hall to her mother's room. Jan walked straight to the far side of the room, to the curtains, to push them open as far as possible, and the sliding glass door, open as far as possible, as if to allow any behavior her mother had left in the room to escape into the yard now. Peach was the prevailing color in the room. Glass flower arrangements sat on either side of her vanity mirror, on the low dresser. A faded peach crocheted throw blanket hung over the end of the peach bedspread, its tassels swaying almost, in the breeze from the open glass door. The wood headboard, the handbags hanging from the coatrack in the corner, it was all as Jan remembered it.

She opened the closet. The clothes, the clothes. The shoes, and the shoeboxes, not filled with shoes, but photographs. Jan knew that. Her mother used to say that they were all packed away in these boxes, so that she could get at them in a fire. Not in photo albums, too heavy to carry if the house was going up in flames. Better to have them all in these boxes, so they could easily be carried out. Jan looked down at one of the many boxes and flipped the lid off with her foot. It looked like the photos were from when Jan was a baby. Jan squatted and pushed the photos around with one finger, not willing to put her whole hand in and fall into a well of reminiscence. She had a whole house to sort through still. She picked up one photo and looked at it closely. That was how she remembered her mother, how she looked, before that first face-lift. The bird, the crane, the swan. Jan looked a moment more and then quickly put it back in the box and replaced the lid.

She'd take these, she supposed, the shoeboxes full of photos. The dresses she'd donate. The furniture could be sold with the house. She didn't want any of it. The photos would come, she supposed they had to. She didn't want to look at them now, but maybe later, look at memories her brain had long ago written over with new information, like a computer cleaning out and deleting files you hardly ever used.

Like that. The memories were imprinted clearly in the photos, though, as if saved on some microchip. Every smell and emotion waiting patiently on each photo to miraculously retrieve memories Jan's mind had obscured with different experiences. Miraculously restore all the information.

Jan piled three shoeboxes in her arms and walked back down the hall. Maybe it wouldn't be so bad, to retrieve those memories, the ones where Jan recognized her mother's face. She put the boxes down by the front door and walked back to her mother's room for more. It might be nice to be reminded of that, and then for the memory of her mother to stay there.

Jan pulled three more boxes into her arms and looked at what was left in the closet. She'd have to come back two more times for the rest of the boxes. Out into the hall, another pile by the front door. And another, and another. She looked at all the boxes on the gray slate floor of the entranceway and felt her willingness to sort through the rest of her mother's things drain from her. She looked around behind her, the living room, the kitchen. It would be fine to leave it all here, right?

Just after her mother's death, one of her mother's friends had sent Jan a recent photo of her, one of her mother's last pictures. She was in a chair at a restaurant, a birthday party, maybe. And Jan didn't know who she was looking at. Her mother had had another face-lift, obviously, another one that Jan didn't know about. When had that happened? Recently? A few years ago? Jan had talked to her mother on the phone every couple of months, usually, and her mother never mentioned it. Hadn't seen her mother in a while, Jan lived too far away for that, really. Couldn't spare the expense. But the phone calls seemed to be all right, Jan thought they were all right. Had her mother felt shame about the second face-lift and not mentioned it, because of that? Or was the second face-lift another demonstration of her instability?

Jan didn't know any of it. After looking at the photo, Jan had immediately torn it up. Jan didn't recognize the woman.

43

Isabella. 97. Wife.
Georgia. 41. Receptionist.

Isabella grew up in a small European town. A forest pressed on the back of the hamlet, pine trees
shoulder to shoulder, sunlight confetti through their
needles, the sounds (and furtive sights) of nightjar
birds and cuckoos, barn owls and finches. Deer and
forest dormice, and even the tiniest shrew. Butter-
cups, blue trumpet flowers, and purple thistles. This
was Isabella's forest.

The ocean opened at the other side of town. Rock
grottoes and seashore caves, turquoise water and sea
foam breezes. Gulls and cranes, loons and skimmers.
Stone crabs and starfish on the shore, more in the
ocean. Pink-bloom sunrises and tangerine-fire sun-
sets. This was Isabella's seashore.

Isabella's town was beautiful as well. Gray pebble
streets and golden limestone buildings. Green-bottle
bottom windows and heather-blue shutters. This
was Isabella's town.

And there was contentment in Isabella's town,
the people around her happy and satisfied. Good
food from the forest and the sea, beautiful things to

look at—beauty all around Isabella. And so, she felt beautiful too. She looked at beautiful things every day and thought of herself as part of this beauty, a particle of the beautiful being that was the forest and the seaside and the town and its birds and flowers and limestone buildings. This was true of everyone in the town: part of the entire beautiful being.

And when Isabella moved from her town, to a different town, to be with her husband, she brought that identity with her, and she felt beautiful. When she grew older and creases dominated her face, she still felt part of that beautiful town, that beautiful being, and never questioned her own beauty.

Isabella's granddaughter, Georgia, grew up in a small town as well, farther away, in America. Georgia's town was monotone and still, industrial and drab. Wet snow in winter and withering humidity in summer. Beauty did not surround Georgia, not in her town. There was discontent and unhappiness, from the others around Georgia. She could see the beauty in the magazines, though, and on TV. She could see it there. Color was unusual in Georgia's town. Color was imported. Through the advertising that was pasted on the town's few billboards, through the TV, through the magazines that came in the mail, fashion and celebrity and décor, showcasing so many smiling faces, so much happiness, so much color.

Georgia carefully tore out the magazine pages

and taped them on the walls of her room when she was a teen, to surround herself with beautiful things, to live there, instead. She wanted to be there, and not in her town. She didn't want to feel included in so much steel, and dripping weather, and the sunken moods of other people. Being in that town made Georgia assume an ugliness, that she was a particle of the being of that place. She would look in the mirror and try to approximate the faces and poses of those people in the magazines and on TV, to be a particle of that instead.

When Georgia got older, her smooth face was replaced with one that was creased and loose and not at all one that could be a particle of the beautiful being in the magazines and on TV. Georgia thought she more definitely looked like part of the gray and sweaty streets and buildings and mood of her town. And this was too much for Georgia to take. She saved her money and bought the treatments that the beautiful people spoke about in magazines and on TV, to get there, to be inside that beautiful being, to feel she was there. And after she'd gotten the fillers and the Botox and her face sanded and pricked with pins and washed with acid to "wake up the collagen in her skin," Georgia looked in the mirror and again tried to approximate the looks and the poses of those she assumed were in the beautiful being, and felt nothing. And she realized that none of those colorful and shiny people were in the beautiful being either.

In the past, she had dismissed her grandmother's old and creased face and those of other
happy, wrinkled-faced people, but now she realized
they were in the beautiful being, they were in there.
And Georgia wanted Isabella to tell her how to get
through the door.

44

Sycamore. 65. The Goethals Library Tree.

When small, the wire.
The guide, support.
Around my waist. To help, to support.
Strong wire, green rubber pad around my waist.
To help. They thought I needed. Maybe not
   needed.

I grew. I was strong. The wind against my length,
   building me.
My resistance against the wind, building me.
I was strong. The support stayed.
Didn't need the support. The fit around my waist
   too much.

I grew, had to grow, couldn't abate the growth,
   did not want to abate the growth.
I grew around it. I could not stop changing, I
   changed around it.
I changed and the support could not.

I grew around it, bulging over the top of the support
   on my waist, below the support on my waist.

Engulfing the support, but not erasing it.

Always showing (cannot hide) the inflexible, unchanging support under that which was strong, after all.

Never able to erase, or start again the growth without the support, to grow (after all) strong and straight.

Ever the growth of the strong, over the unchanging support.

A lump, a bulge of fear that I would not grow, could not grow, strong and straight.

Fear that the wind, that tossed me to and fro, would destroy me.

The wind was to build me.

They didn't know. They forgot.

The face, the face I see at the base of the tree, on the bench.

A face on a person, sitting on the bench.

The face with something in it, a support, something inside of it.

An insertion of something, a change, a cut, something to support.

A face that could grow straight and strong like me. Like I could have without the support.

A straight and strong face, but not now.

A support that the face will grow around, must grow around.

The face will grow and not stop, change and not
   stop.
Change around the unchangeable, the support,
   that they didn't need.
Like me. Like I didn't need.
The fear, the fear I would not grow strong and
   straight.

The face will grow around the fear and not be the
   same.
It will not be what it could have been, knowing
   the wind would build and not destroy.
Instead, still grow, and bulge over and under the
   support.
It didn't need.

45

Maggie. 54. Lawyer.

Dear Actresses of the 1960s, '70s, and early '80s,
I never noticed your wrinkles.

I never pulled that bit of information from your image on the screen or the television. I never noticed lines or bags under your eyes.

I was a child, I was a teen, then a young woman.

I never noticed. Not then, not when you got older. I didn't see that.

I could see your attitude, how you handled situations, how you walked, how you dressed. How you sat in a chair or drove a car. How you expressed anger, triumph, tragedy. There were other women in my life to watch, but you were beyond.

Diane Keaton, Julie Christie, Jacqueline Bisset, Carol Kane, Ellen Burstyn, Madeline Kahn, Shelley Duvall, Jill Clayburgh, Eileen Brennan, Cloris Leachman, Teri Garr, Jane Alexander, Shelley Winters, Gena Rowlands, Glenda Jackson, Jeanne Moreau, Candy Clark, Geraldine Page, Charlotte Rampling, Brooke Adams, Maggie Smith, Geneviève Bujold, Anne Bancroft, Lois Chiles, Joyce Van Patten, Louise Fletcher, Peggy Lipton, Joanne Woodward, Lee Grant, Julie

Kavner, Jean Stapleton, Bea Arthur, Adrienne Bar-
beau, Marion Ross, Esther Rolle, Linda Lavin, Mary
Kay Place, and more. You were beyond what I could
witness in the women around me, in my small reach
into the world.

You stood straight and stared people down. You
had a sword of wit and cut people with that many
times before they even noticed. You set terms with
men you wanted to be with. You wore clothes that
were stylish in ways that are difficult to cultivate. I
saw this. This is the only thing I saw. And so, I wanted
to be like you. I wanted to be a me that could do all
that. Stand straight, and be true, and hold people off
when they tried to limit my attempts to find the edges.
To dress in a way that telegraphed that. To signal that
I was like you, doing all the things I saw you do. I just
want you to know how important that all was to me.
Because I could see you, those things, I could become my version of it.

But now, I live in a society (and perhaps this was
the same for you and I never knew it) that focuses so
manically on the literal landscape of a woman's face,
negatively broadcasting the millimeters of change in
the tautness of the skin on her face, her neck, around
her eyes. Creases and bags and dark circles. Not
looking at the person, but at the arrangement of skin
on her face. So much so that I feel like I can't breathe
anymore. I want to say, "But look what I've achieved!
Look how I've ingested all these freeing and superb

signals from those women who went before. See
them emanate from me now. See that."

I don't know how we got here, but it's seeped
into my blood. When I watch you now, the films and
TV shows of yours that I used to look at, I can see
your lines and your bags. I see the creases and the
jowls. How can I see that now? How did I never see it
before? I feel ashamed that my blood has been polluted with this awareness, that this blood circulates
in my brain now and pokes me with its finger to take
note of your faces. And I feel sick with the knowledge
that millions of young women, the ages I was before
when I saw you and was bolstered by ingesting your
signals, will be blocked from ingesting similar signals.
Their blood has been poisoned too, and their brains
are poking them to notice it on others, to notice it on
themselves.

But it's not just their blood and brains that have
been poisoned. They are doubly cursed. It's also polluted the brains of the older woman (like me) who
are now supposed to be sending them the types of
signals you all once sent me. So, now no one signaling, and no one able to see the signals. Like a
grand mummification of the freedom of expression
we women are destined for. It's like we've all been
tricked into shuttering our progress, into making us
terrified of someone seeing our wrinkles and bags.
And for what? What exactly does a woman get for
shutting down the signals of a free and strong life in

favor of an expressionless and baby-smooth face?

They're simply trying to kill us and I don't know why we're going along with the plan.

Yours,
Maggie Truman

46

Woman. 3.

When I was little I had a face. I didn't think about my face. I used it to create expressions to elicit reactions from others. That's what my face was for, just a tool. But I never thought about my face.

Woman. 12.

People would comment to my parents that I was a pretty girl. They seemed to have to say that, as if not saying it would be shockingly rude to my parents. I don't think I was any more or less pretty than any other girls my age. But it seemed to be the best, most high compliment you could pay a girl. That she was pretty. It seemed to be a very low bar or an unattainable one, depending on how people regarded you. You could either qualify for this "pretty girl" accomplishment and have nothing more required of you (and in fact be criticized for trying to augment that with any true accomplishments), or you could be forever trying to compensate for not being regarded as pretty with untold accomplishments, always falling short of that pinnacle accomplishment of being a pretty girl.

Woman. 17.

I now knew I had fulfilled my contract with society. I was confirmed a "pretty girl" by its standards. I didn't have to do anything else. I could die now and society would feel satisfied that I had completed my potential. I had reached the highest expectation for a female. I was a welcome addition to any group setting because of that. I was a desirable mate because of that. I was a success, and hadn't done anything yet.

Woman. 24.

Using the currency society had given me with its "pretty girl" accolade, I spent freely. I enjoyed the marketplace in which I had spending power. I was careful to highlight my pretty girl title, as to not seem ungrateful for the prize. I was also careful to not excel too publicly or loudly. After all, it didn't seem like any accomplishment besides being regarded as a pretty girl would get me further in life, anyway.

Woman. 30.

Having no great investment in my looks, as they seemed to have mattered to others far more than they mattered to me, I began to expand. I looked more closely at other things. Literature, philosophy, ambition, passion, strife. I no longer dedicated attention to my "pretty girl" title, and ignored its value. Society may have felt shunned, and felt that I was ungrateful, but I was weary of appreciating the position any longer.

Woman. 39.

After a great deal of accomplishments and attention for my efforts in the world, I became aware of a vein of spitefulness directed at me. I know I broke that contract with society wherein I would be awarded the "pretty girl" title, and in return I would not thumb my nose at it by striving to achieve anything greater. For to strive to achieve anything greater is to demonstrate that there are more valuable things than the pretty girl title. Telling society that their highest accolade is not, has its repercussions.

Woman. 45.

I had my title pulled from me. The "pretty girl" title was revoked. Of course, many would have argued that I was still pretty or attractive, but I know society recalled what it had given me before. The title can be revoked, of course. It was to be expected. I did not demonstrate the gratitude necessary to retain the title for the maximum amount of time. I had played loosely with it. I wore makeup infrequently. I achieved things beyond the title, an aggressive demonstration of my lack of appreciation for it. I also looked older, another sign of my ungratefulness for having been labeled a pretty girl. More offensively, I did not "fix" my face when it started getting older, with fillers and peels and toxins and knives and all the other means by which you demonstrate that you value the pretty girl title. And I was punished for it.

Woman. 50.

I was very clearly aware of the young women who currently had the title. I saw them move through stores, walk down streets, drive their cars, talk with their friends. The ones with the title. They knew it, like I knew it before. However, they hadn't yet broken their agreement with society. They were holding the title up as the highest achievement. They were honoring that.

I hadn't realized what that title had given me before. I took it for granted. I saw that, when the title was revoked. I felt the loss. The confidence, the insouciance. I often saw myself the way society saw me there, and I shouldn't have. It wanted me to feel less than I was when I had the title. It wanted me to feel like I now had no worth, like I was a body moving through the air, with an older face, a less necessary face. A body taking up space, and valued only at the most base level. That I had worth as a human being, but that is it. That if I had been killed, society wouldn't have felt the loss the way they would if I had still been a pretty girl, but the police would have investigated the homicide of this woman with a now cracked and creased and loose-skinned face. Not quite, but almost. They'd still investigate because I still qualified as a human being, and by God, we aren't animals.

Woman. 53.
I did something illegal, but that could not be stopped. Society was furious, but couldn't change what I did. I gave the title to myself. Not in the superficial measure that society gives the title, but I awarded myself the results of that title. The confidence, the fearlessness that everything will go my way, eventually. That's what that "pretty girl" title gave me before, I realized. I'm sure they don't want anyone to know that, that the confidence can be grabbed without the title being bestowed upon you.

Woman. 65.
I took a bath in that confidence. Drinking it, rubbing it in my hair, on my body. I still felt society trying to press that "worthlessness" label upon me, in order to maintain some macabre consistency among themselves. It became faint, though. The confidence became a habit. Everywhere I went, everyone with whom I spoke. It was free of any opinions of me, free of any societal titles, free of anyone else's capriciousness. Sometimes I saw others notice it, in that somewhat startled way, and I wanted to give it to them too. But I know I can't give something that no one else can give you.

Woman. 82.
I'll die soon. I don't mind . . . I think about that "pretty

girl" title sometimes. It's a terrible bell jar, meant to capture and prohibit the forward progress of those with a particular appearance. I think society fears that the prettiness is a signal that other exceptional traits lurk beneath the surface and, if given free reign, would overwhelm us all. So, best to trap that butterfly and trick it into feeling that the greatest accomplishment has already been attained. Convince them to look no further, lest the rest of their possible magnificence be released.

At the same time, for those without this pretty girl appearance, the title is the unattainable carrot held above their heads, the striving for it distracting them from exploring what they could achieve, or undermining their confidence in their achievements by always whispering to them that they have yet to reach the pinnacle of female accomplishment, they have yet to be called a "pretty girl."

And right when a woman is old enough to step into her worth and has achieved a significant mark on the world, society tries to make her terrified that she has an older face, no longer a pretty face. That her natural aging face will cause every accomplishment to be ignored.

And that can distract a woman, if she believes it.

47

Justine. 53. Filmmaker and Author.

"You know what you're looking at? You're looking at snow skiing almost every year, weekends at Zuma Beach, vacations to the seashores of Mexico and Brazil and Fiji and Italy and France, thousands of hours of travel through airports and airplanes and trains and taxis. You're looking at birthing two babies and getting up in the middle of the night over and over to feed them and change their dirty sheets and coax them back to bed. You're looking at laughing so hard I couldn't stop the soundless heaves of joy that were too strong to make noise. You're looking at staying out late and dancing until my clothes and my hair were dripping with sweat, and tasting that sweat when I licked my dry lips, lying in my bed later, convincing my body to sleep when it could see the sun rising. You're looking at hundreds of lyrics yelled at a hundred concerts, while lights throbbed around me. You're looking at thousands of applications of foundation and eyeliner and rouge and powder and working so many hours on a film set that the PAs had to wake me to come shoot the last scene. You're seeing the relentless effort behind creating and running a

clothing company and years of knitting creations, almost without ceasing. You're looking at hundreds of
thousands of kisses and the intimacy that only skin
can give to skin. You're looking at thousands and
thousands of hours of tears and necessarily violent
emotional expression that shrugged off the crust of
others and made me free. You're looking at four years
of relentless university study and thousands of hours
of sometimes frustratingly fruitless, then magnifi-
cently triumphant, computer coding. You're seeing
hundreds of singular and razor-focused completions
of performances and poems and scripts and propos-
als and books and films. You're seeing the repeated
expression of incredulity delivered to others' projects
and decisions that were false and lazy. You're looking at fucking determination and truth and creativity.
You're looking at loss and sorrow and the effort for
deeper perspective. You're looking at satisfaction
and happiness. You're looking at the manifestation
of a connection so deep and rooted that it's more
real than I am. You're looking at my face."

Acknowledgments

Thank you to the many women and men I interviewed for this book; I'm honored that you trusted me with your time and your honesty. Thanks to Dr. Andrew Frankel for his time, consultation, and surgical markings on my face for the cover photo. (Dr. Frankel has some of the best "before and after" plastic surgery photos of anyone I researched, by the way.) Thanks to Dr. Rhonda Rand for that introduction.

Thank you to the superior short story writing talents of Joyce Carol Oates, Adam Johnson, Deb Olin Unferth, and Holiday Reinhorn. Thank you to my publisher, Johnny Temple, for his always insightful notes and cooperative methods. Thanks to everyone at Akashic Books for the work before, during, and after publication. Thank you to my book agent, Anthony Arnove, for his enthusiasm and frankness about the work, both the creative and the professional.

Thanks to Marty, Duke, and Gia for being so interesting, funny, and loyal; I love you. Thanks to G.J. for everything. And thank you to Georgia O'Keeffe and all the other confident older women who have worn their age on their faces in sexy defiance. You gave me a look to which I can aspire.

Also available by Justine Bateman from Akashic Books

FAME
The Hijacking of Reality
224 pages. Hardcover, $26.95

"Wholly riveting."
—*New York Times Book Review*

"Revelatory and raucous, fascinating and frightening, *Fame* is a hell of a ride."
—Michael J. Fox, actor, author of *A Funny Thing Happened on the Way to the Future*

"In a new book, the two-time Emmy nominee takes a raw look at the culture of celebrity, reflecting on her stardom at its dizzying peak—and the 'disconcerting' feeling as it began to fade." —*People*

"As the title *Fame: The Hijacking of Reality* more than implies, this is a book about the complicated aspects of all things fame."
—*Vanity Fair*

"Bateman digs into the out-of-control nature of being famous, its psychological aftermath and why we all can't get enough of it."
—*New York Post*

"The *Family Ties* alum has written the rawest, bleakest book on fame you're ever likely to read. Bateman's close-up of the celeb experience features vivid encounters with misogyny, painful meditations on aging in Hollywood, and no shortage of theses on social media's wrath."
—*Entertainment Weekly*

"Bateman addresses the reader directly, pouring out her thoughts in a rapid-fire, conversational style. (Hunter S. Thompson is saluted in the acknowledgments.) . . . But her jittery delivery suits the material—the manic sugar high of celebrity and its inevitable crash. Bateman takes the reader through her entire fame cycle, from TV megastar, whose first movie role was alongside Julia Roberts, to her quieter life today as a filmmaker. She is as relentless with herself as she is with others." —*Washington Post*